Great Lies to tell Small Kids

Andy Riley is the author of THE BOOK OF BUNNY SUICIDES and RETURN OF THE BUNNY SUICIDES. He has written for Black Books, Little Britain, Smack The Pony, Trigger Happy TV, Big Train and The Armando Iannucci Shows. He is the co-creator of Hyperdrive, BBC2's new science fiction sitcom, and Radio 4's The 99p Challenge. His weekly cartoon strip, Roasted, runs in the Observer Magazine.

Great Lies to tell Small Kids

Andy Riley

HODDER &
STOUGHTON

First published in Great Britain in 2005 by Hodder and Stoughton
A division of Hodder Headline

A Hodder & Stoughton book

1 3 5 7 9 10 8 6 4 2

A CIP catalogue record for this title is available from the British Library

Hardback ISBN 0 340 83405 6
Paperback ISBN 0 340 83406 4

Printed and bound in Spain by Book Print, S. L.

Hodder Headline's policy is to use papers that are natural, renewable and recyclable products and made from wood grown in sustainable forests. The logging and manufacturing processes are expected to conform to the environmental regulations of the country of origin

Hodder and Stoughton Ltd
A division of Hodder Headline
338 Euston Road
London NW1 3BH

With thanks to:
Polly Faber, Camilla Hornby, Nick Davies
and all at Hodder & Stoughton,
Kevin Cecil, Armando Iannucci

Rain is Jesus's wee-wee

THERE'S NO SUCH THING AS KANGAROOS THEY'RE JUST MICE STANDING VERY NEAR

MOUSE

"KANGAROO"

WINE

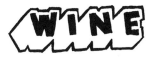

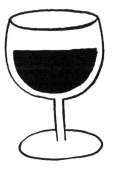

MAKES MUMMY
CLEVER

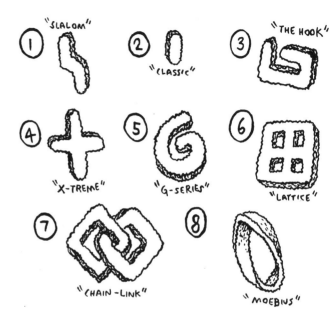

1 "SLALOM"

2 "CLASSIC"

3 "THE HOOK"

4 "X-TREME"

5 "G-SERIES"

6 "LATTICE"

7 "CHAIN-LINK"

8 "MOEBIUS"

WHEN I WAS YOUR
AGE WEETABIX CAME
IN EIGHT DIFFERENT
SHAPES

POLICEMEN GROW FROM HELMETS IN A SINGLE NIGHT ᔐ

IT'S UNLUCKY NOT TO NAME EVERY ANT YOU SEE

DAVE
DARREN MOBUTU
ALISON CROSS
TOSTIG
EL GORDO
TESS
MRS. ANTY
KARL HUGHES
JOHNNY SPOONS
ROBERT SHANNON
FUNKATEER
MOUSEMAT
TIM
HANNIBAL
SUPRIYA
KATH
JELENA
FACE-MAN
PAUL
DON VAN VLIET
MR. COBBETT
ELSIE MACKAY
ASHRAF

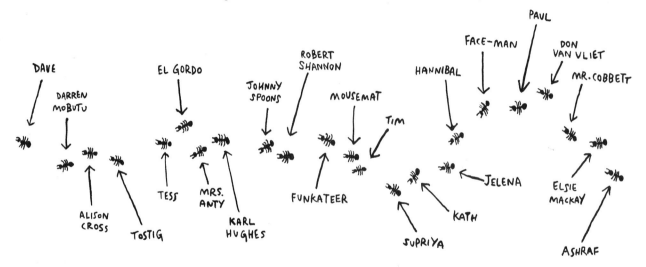

FOR YOUR WHOLE LIFE

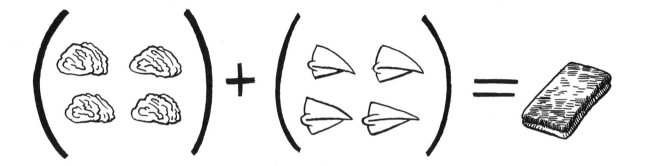

IT TAKES THE BRAINS AND
BEAKS OF FOUR REAL PENGUINS
TO MAKE ONE PENGUIN
BISCUIT

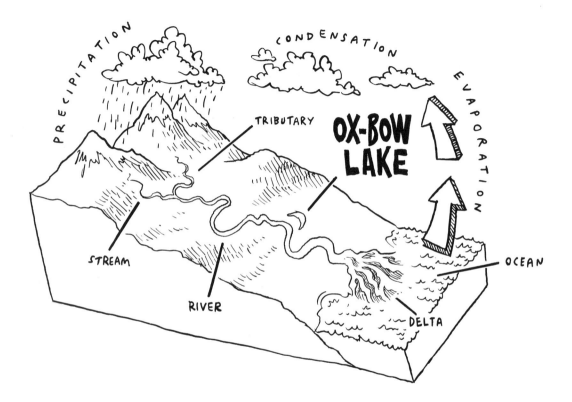

PRECIPITATION

CONDENSATION

EVAPORATION

TRIBUTARY

OX-BOW LAKE

STREAM

RIVER

DELTA

OCEAN

WHEN THEY TEACH YOU THE WATER CYCLE AT SCHOOL, MAKE SURE YOU REMEMBER THE BIT ABOUT **OX-BOW LAKES.** YOU'LL COME ACROSS THEM A **LOT** IN LATER LIFE.

MILK FEELS PAIN

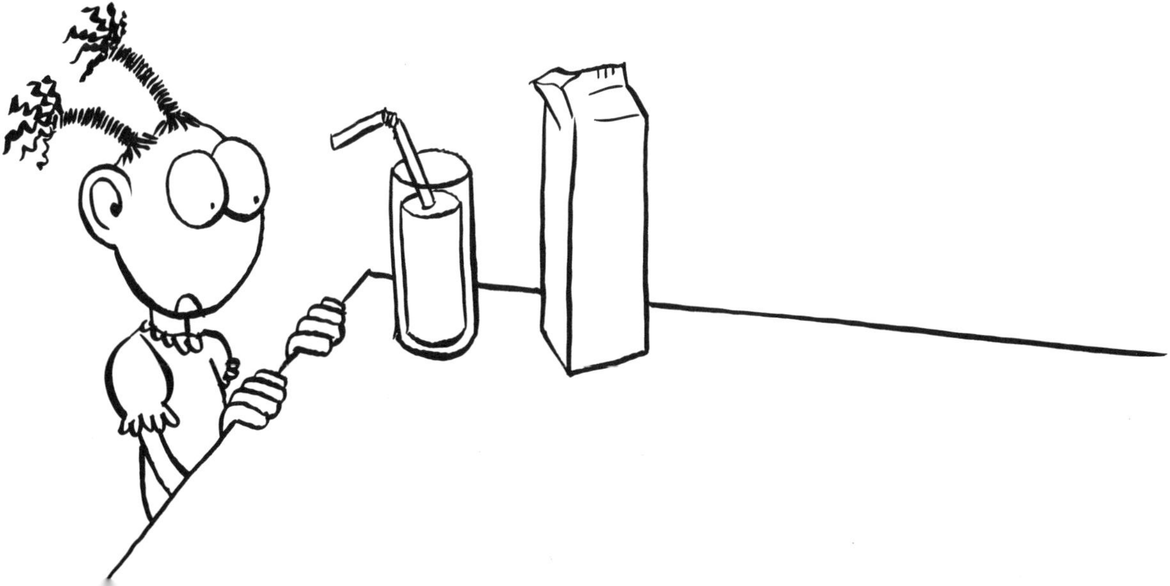

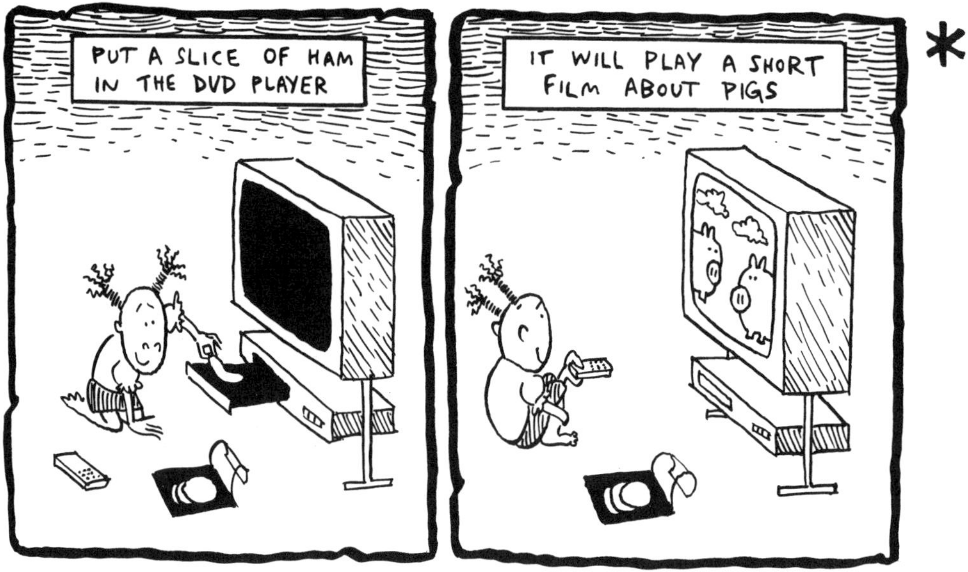
PUT A SLICE OF HAM IN THE DVD PLAYER
IT WILL PLAY A SHORT FILM ABOUT PIGS
*

* A SLICE OF CHEESE WILL PLAY A SHORT FILM ABOUT COWS

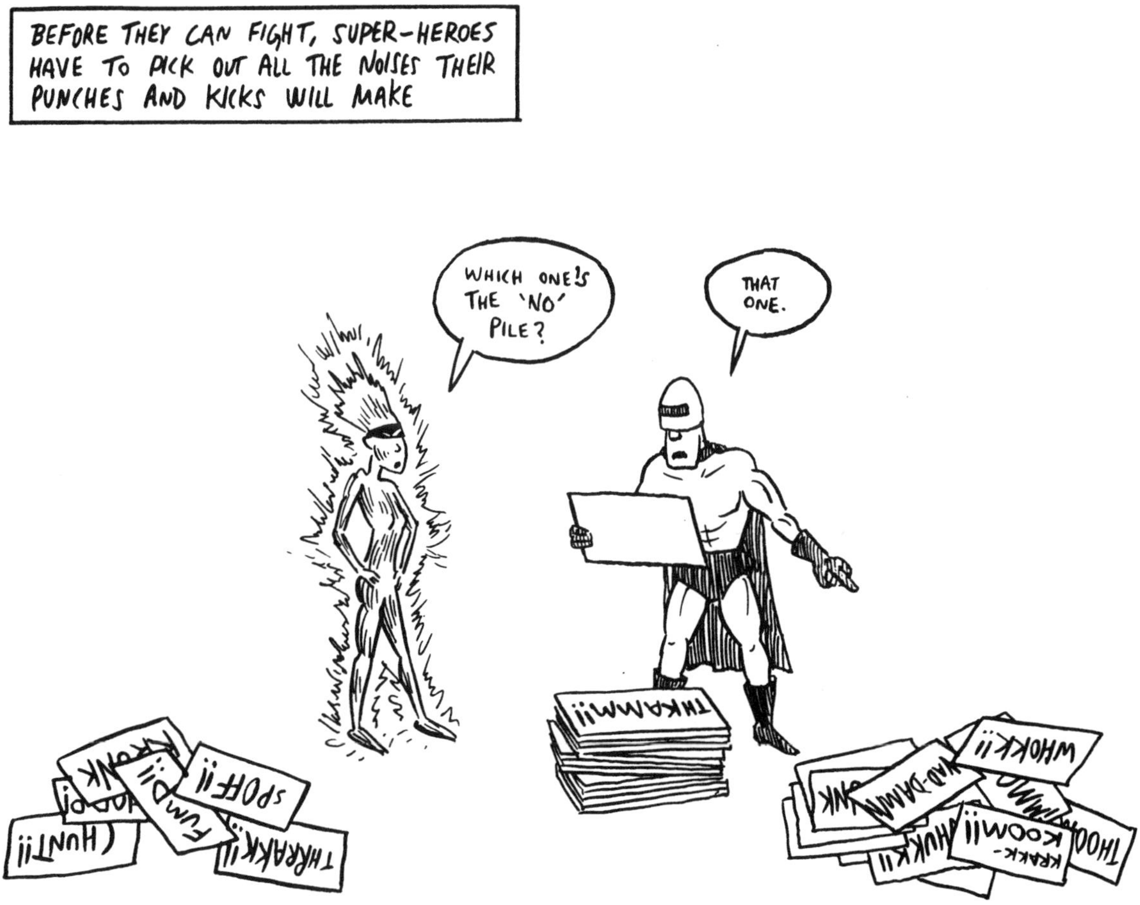
BEFORE THEY CAN FIGHT, SUPER-HEROES HAVE TO PICK OUT ALL THE NOISES THEIR PUNCHES AND KICKS WILL MAKE
WHICH ONE'S THE 'NO' PILE?
THAT ONE.
THKAMM!!
WHOKK!!
SPOFF!!
THRAKK!!
KRAKK-KOOM!!

STRICTLY SPEAKING, THE TOMATO
IS NOT A VEGETABLE

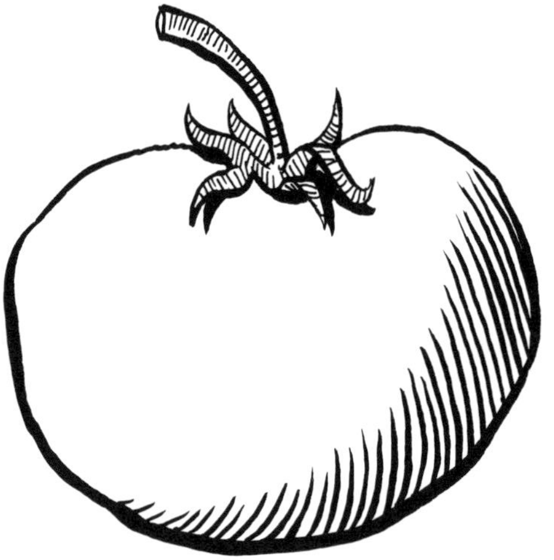

IT'S REALLY A KIND OF DOLPHIN

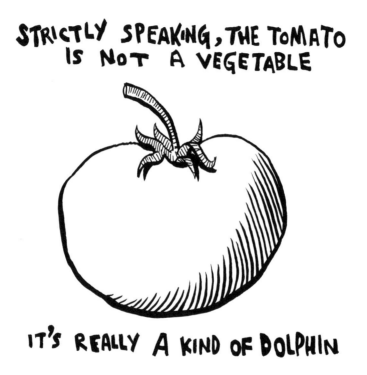

THERE'S A DIRECTOR'S CUT OF "THE SOUND OF MUSIC" WITH A DIFFERENT ENDING

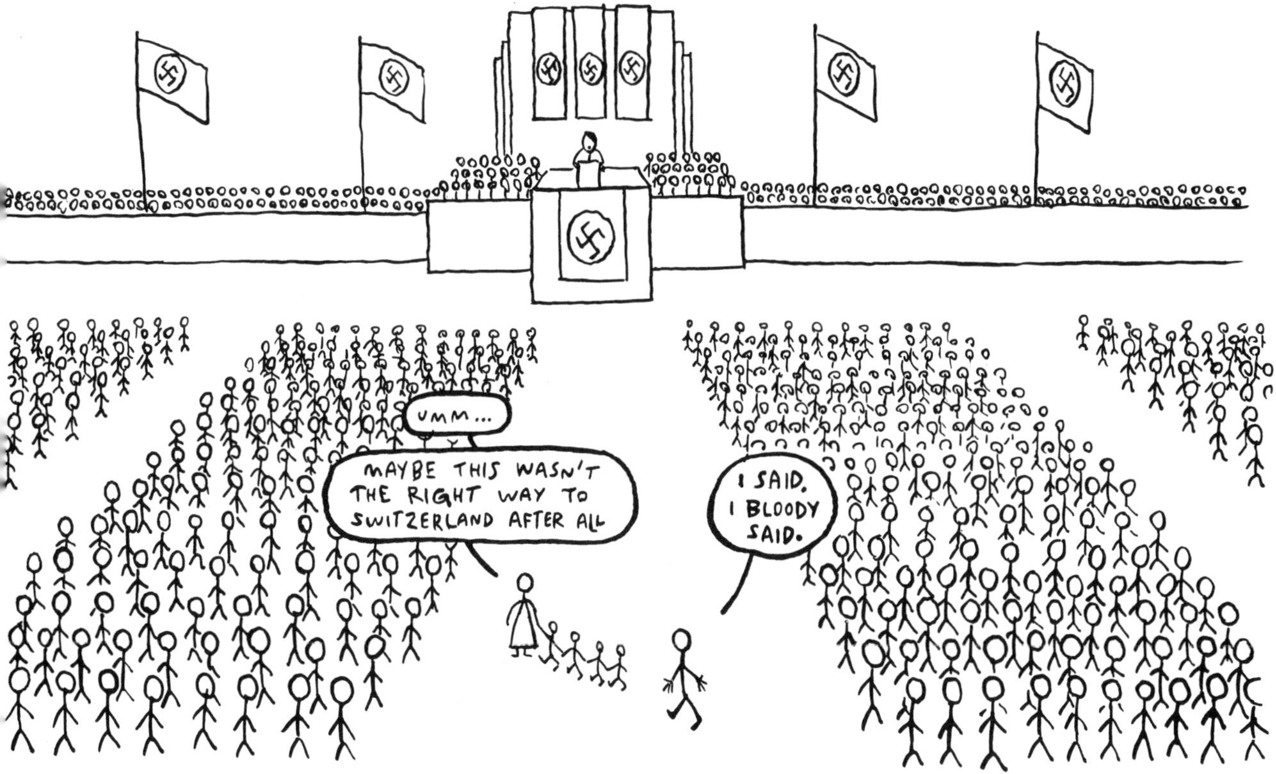
UMM...
MAYBE THIS WASN'T THE RIGHT WAY TO SWITZERLAND AFTER ALL
I SAID. I BLOODY SAID.

THE CAN OPENER WAS
INVENTED 98 YEARS
BEFORE THE CAN

ONE IN TEN FISH ARE AFRAID OF WATER

LIONS CARRY BARCODE SCANNERS

THEY RUN THEM OVER ZEBRAS TO CHECK HOW MUCH THEY COST BEFORE THEY EAT THEM

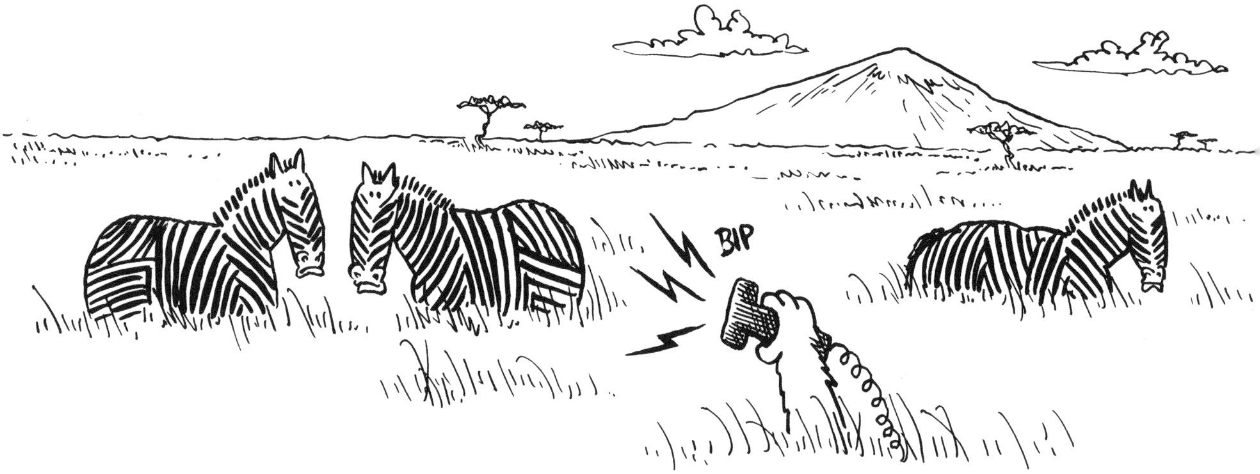
BIP

MEN DON'T GO BALD NATURALLY

THEY JUST LIKE GETTING THEIR HAIR CUT THAT WAY

the victorians forgot to have the year 1862

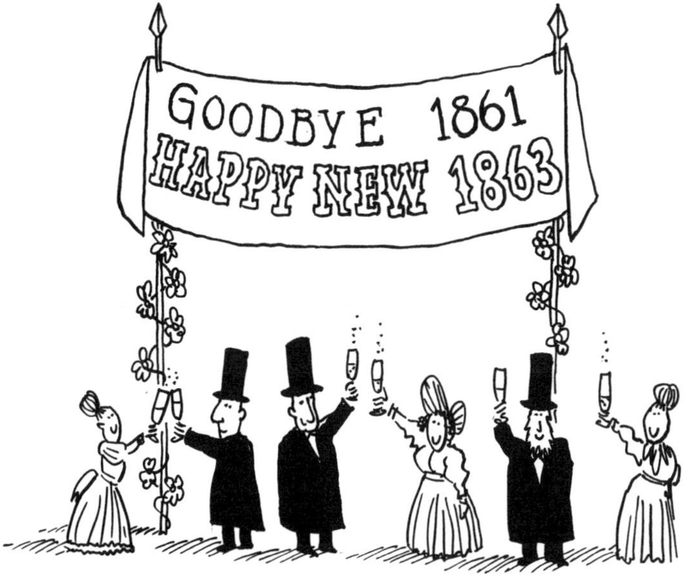
GOODBYE 1861
HAPPY NEW 1863

› the error went unnoticed for more than a century

› the year was finally held between 1995 and 1996

MICE COLLECT YOUR DANDRUFF
AND EAT IT AS CORNFLAKES

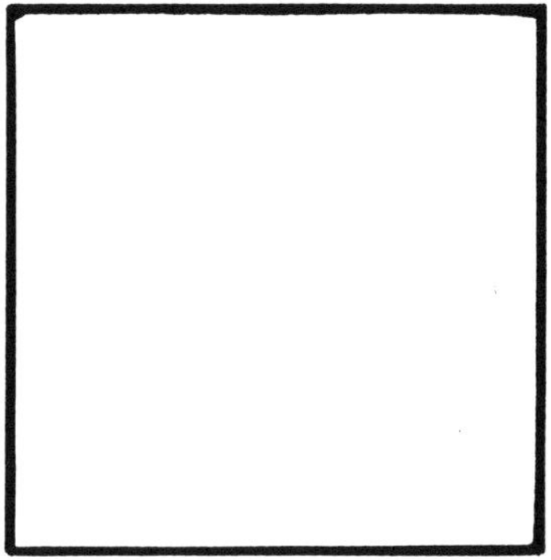

THIS SQUARE HAS A SECRET
FIFTH SIDE WHICH YOU WILL
ONLY SEE IF YOU STARE
AT IT FOR A VERY VERY
VERY LONG TIME

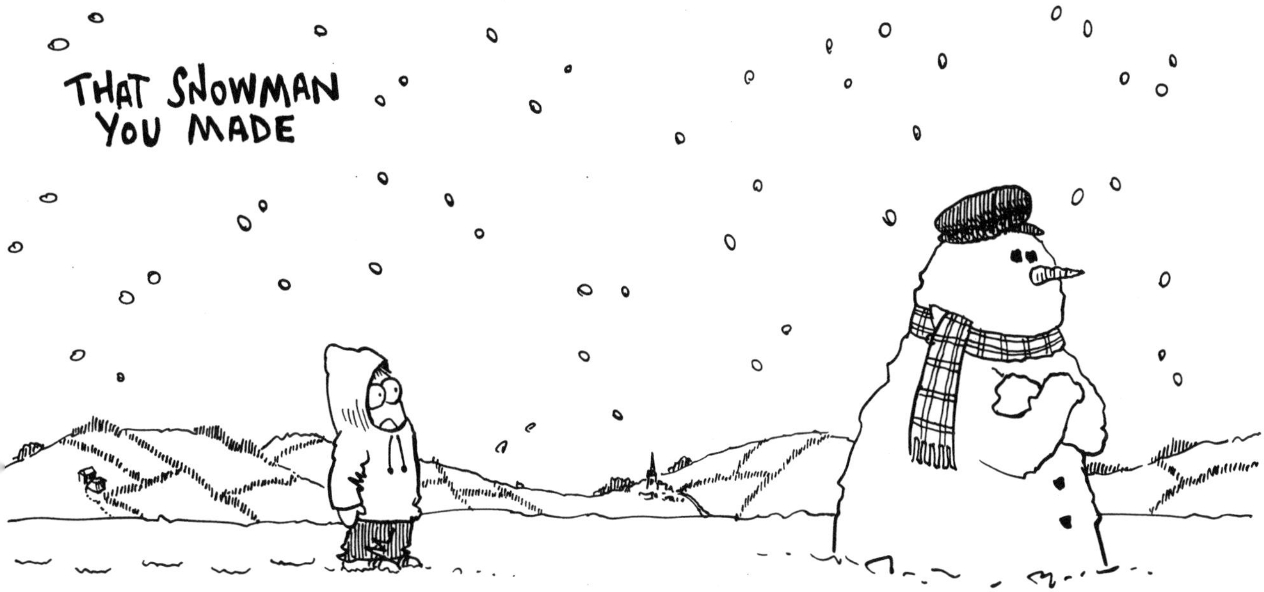
THAT SNOWMAN
YOU MADE

HE SAYS HE WON'T GO WALKING IN THE AIR WITH YOU 'COS YOU'RE A STUPID BENNY

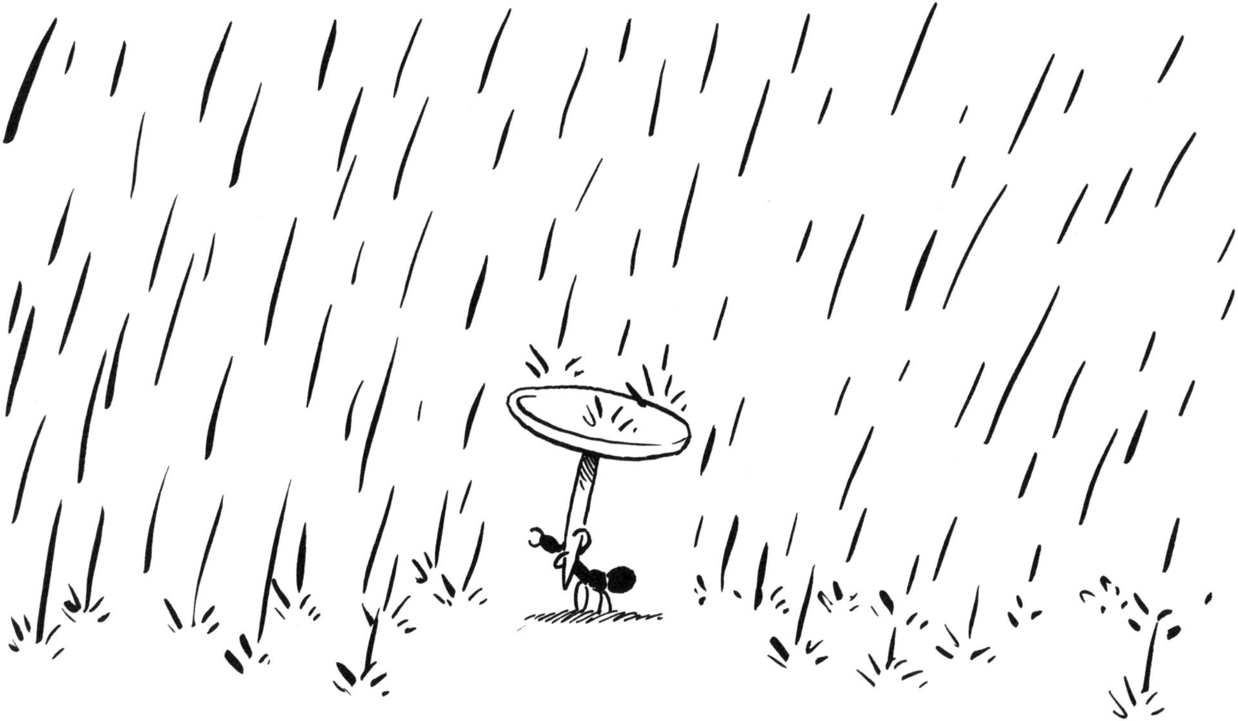

SCATTER DRAWING PINS NEXT TO AN ANTS' NEST
THEN WAIT TILL IT RAINS
THEY'LL PICK THEM UP AND USE THEM AS UMBRELLAS

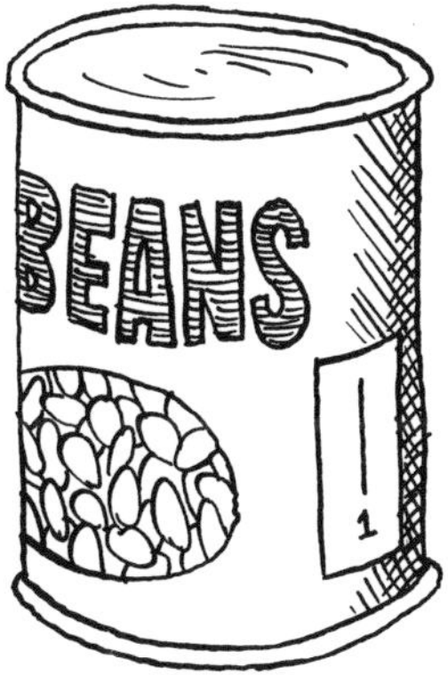
BEANS
1

BAR CODES WERE SIMPLER IN THE OLD DAYS

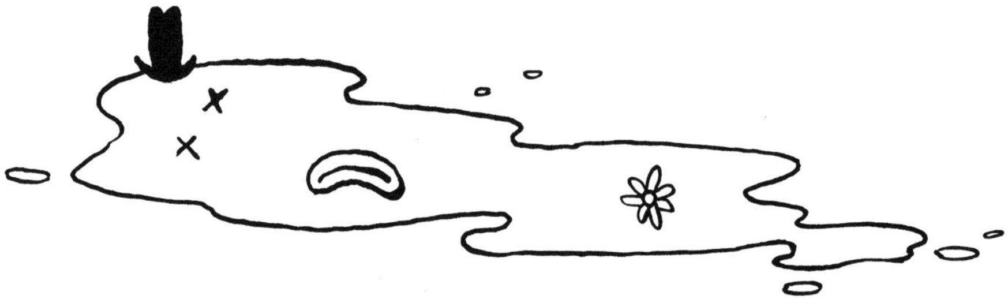

CLOWNS MELT AT 29°C

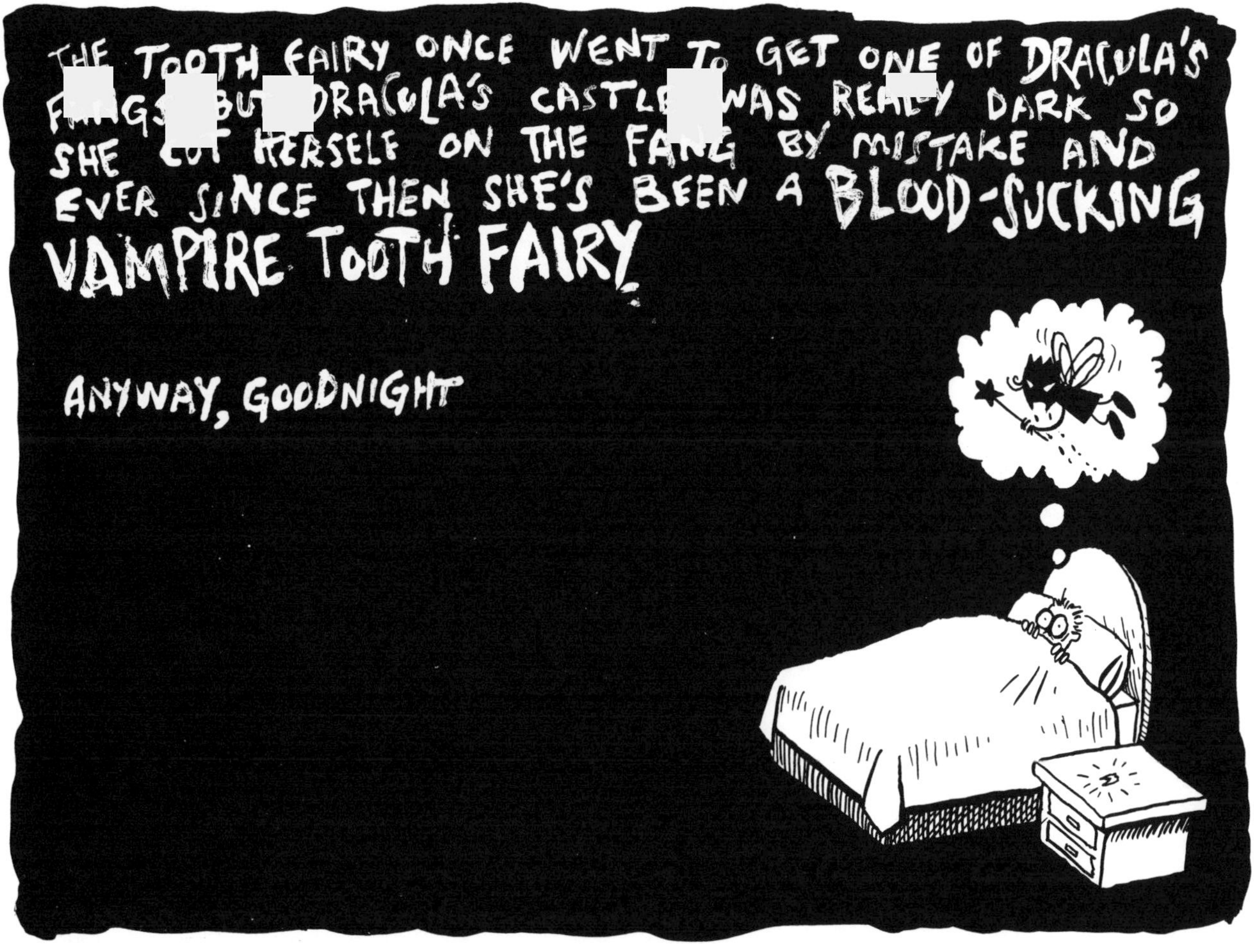
THE TOOTH FAIRY ONCE WENT TO GET ONE OF DRACULA'S F[redacted]GS[redacted]BU[redacted]RACULA'S CASTLE[redacted]WAS RE[redacted]Y DARK SO SHE [redacted] HERSELF ON THE FA[redacted] BY MISTAKE AND EVER SINCE THEN SHE'S BEEN A BLOOD-SUCKING VAMPIRE TOOTH FAIRY.
ANYWAY, GOODNIGHT

THAT WORD DAD
USES SOMETIMES

IT MEANS "PLEASE"

USE IT IN SCHOOL
AND AT THE SHOPS

MUGS ARE JUST CUPS WHO'VE BEEN TO THE GYM

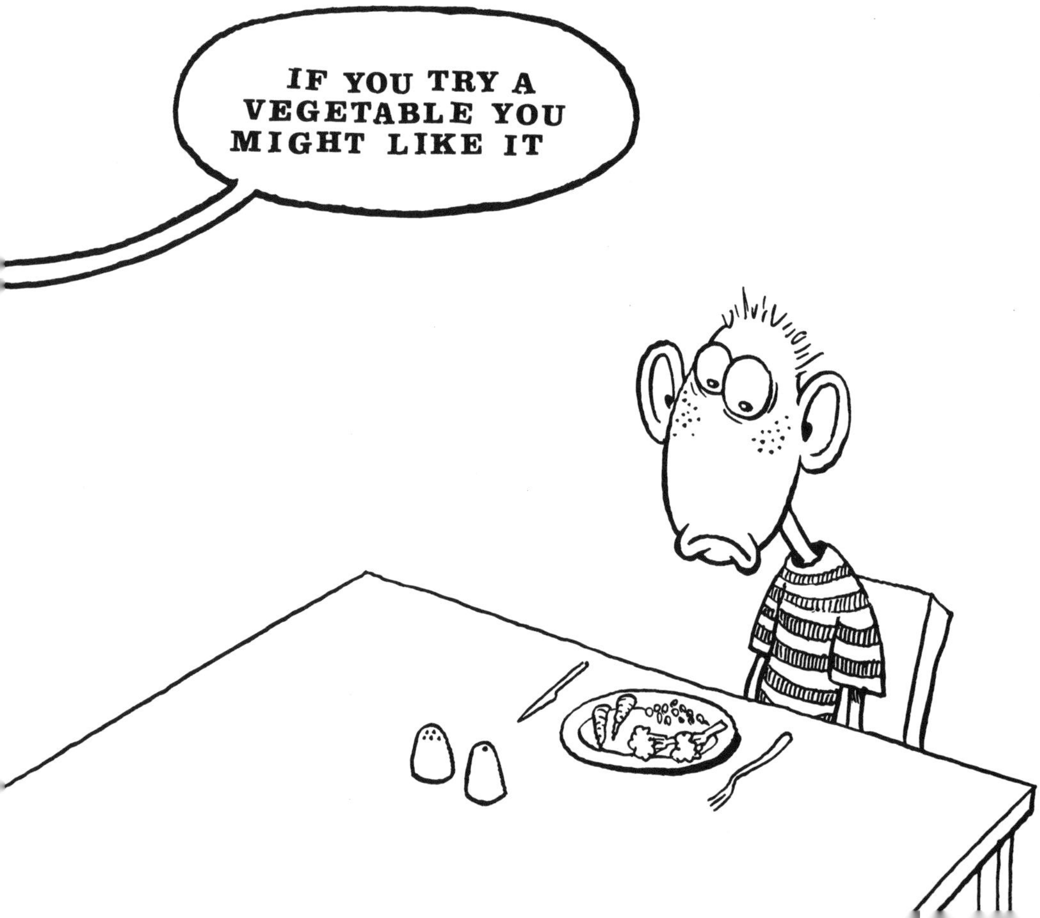
IF YOU TRY A VEGETABLE YOU MIGHT LIKE IT

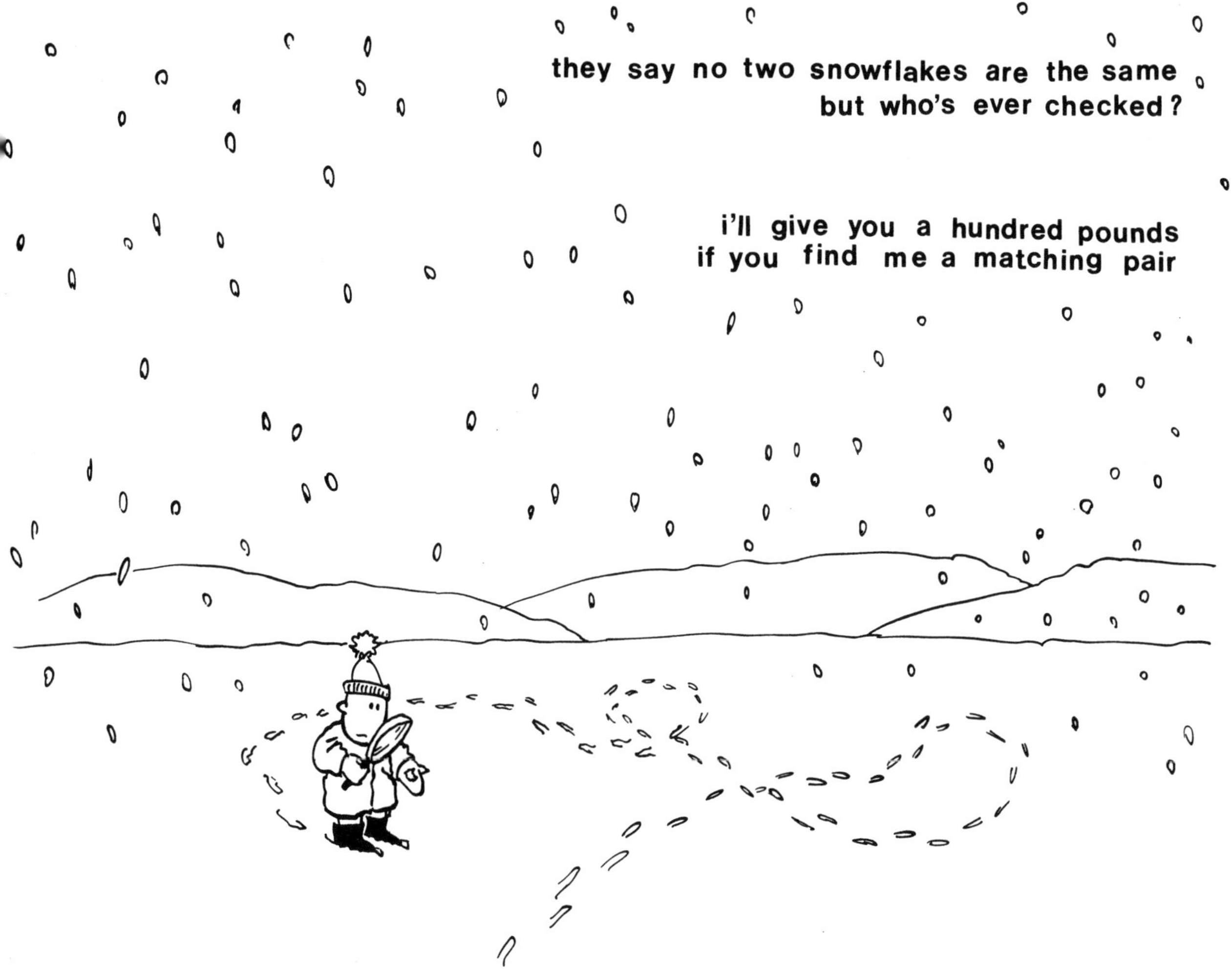
they say no two snowflakes are the same
but who's ever checked?
i'll give you a hundred pounds
if you find me a matching pair

penguins spend a lot of time wondering why pixar have never made a film about them

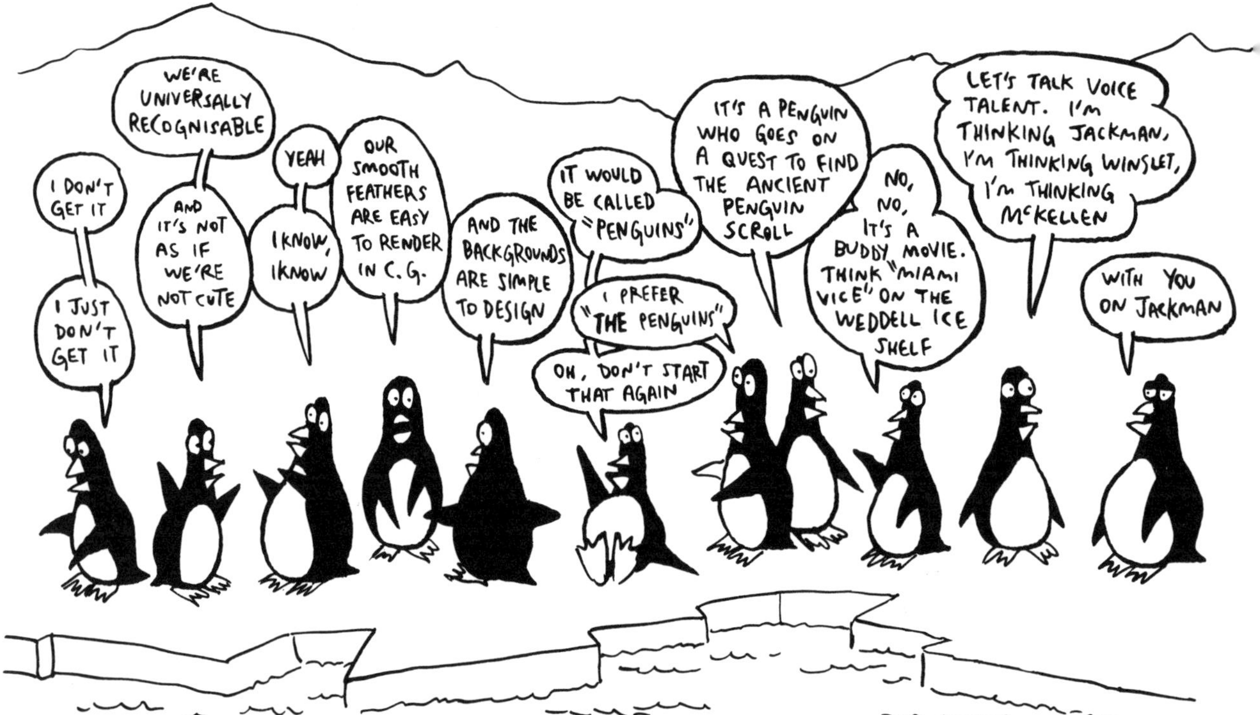
I DON'T GET IT
I JUST DON'T GET IT
WE'RE UNIVERSALLY RECOGNISABLE
AND IT'S NOT AS IF WE'RE NOT CUTE
YEAH
I KNOW, I KNOW
OUR SMOOTH FEATHERS ARE EASY TO RENDER IN C.G.
AND THE BACKGROUNDS ARE SIMPLE TO DESIGN
IT WOULD BE CALLED "PENGUINS"
I PREFER "THE PENGUINS"
OH, DON'T START THAT AGAIN
IT'S A PENGUIN WHO GOES ON A QUEST TO FIND THE ANCIENT PENGUIN SCROLL
NO, NO, IT'S A BUDDY MOVIE. THINK "MIAMI VICE" ON THE WEDDELL ICE SHELF
LET'S TALK VOICE TALENT. I'M THINKING JACKMAN, I'M THINKING WINSLET, I'M THINKING McKELLEN
WITH YOU ON JACKMAN

GODZILLA HAS EVERY FRIDAY OFF

ALL WIND IS MADE BY WIND FARMS

IN DENMARK
THEY USE BACON
AS BANK NOTES

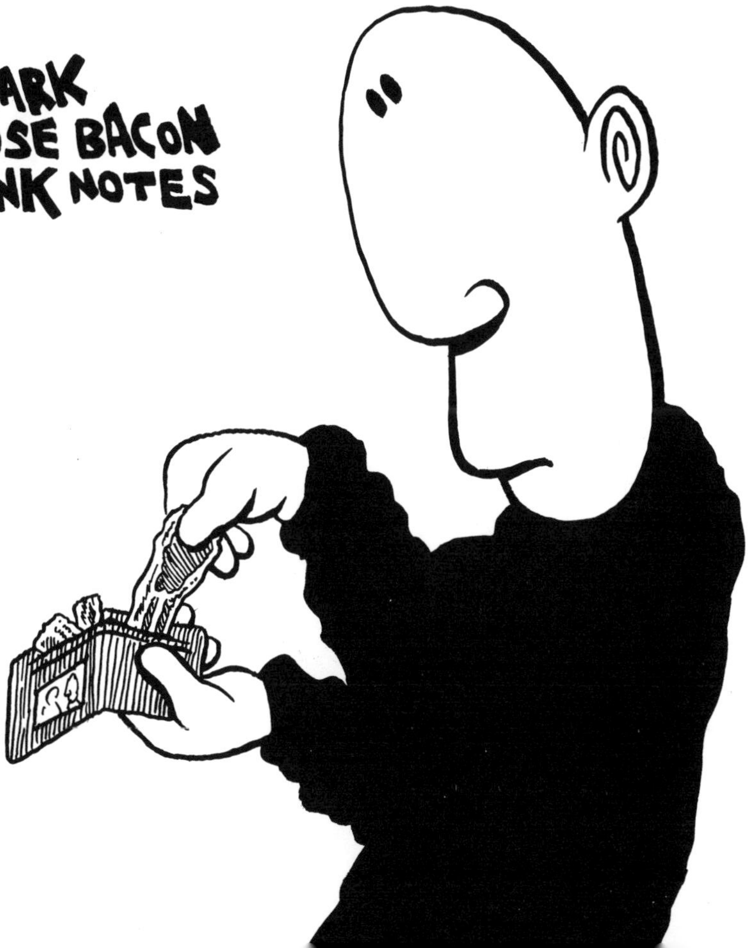

BEWARE OF GUITARS

A SMALL HAIRY PRIMATE CALLED A "WARRIS" LIVES INSIDE EVERY ONE

THEY LIVE ON A DIET OF HUMAN FINGERS

IF YOU GRAB THE EDGE
OF YOUR CHAIR AND
PULL AS HARD AS YOU
CAN YOU'LL LIFT YOURSELF
INTO THE AIR

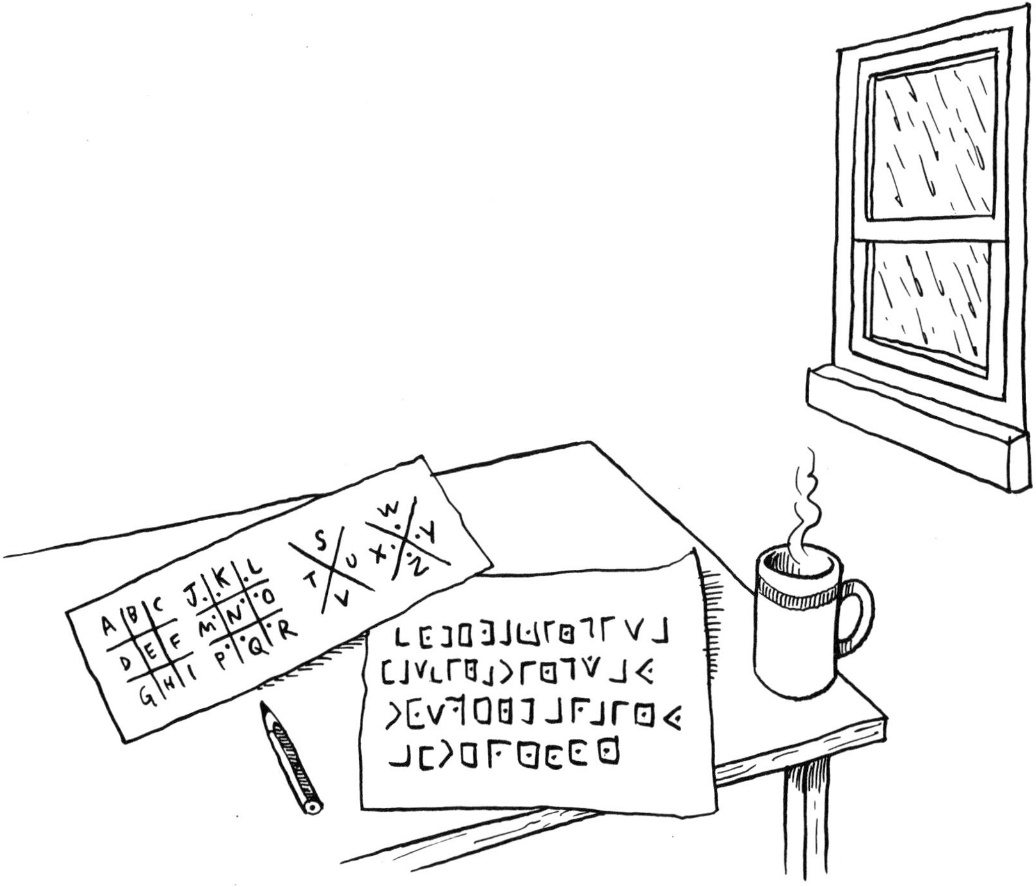
A B C D E F G H I
J K L M N O P Q R
S T U V
W X Y Z

IT WAS GRANDAD WHO BURNED ALL YOUR BARNEY VIDEOS

NOT US

PUBS HAVE SPECIAL MAGNETS WHICH DRAG DAD IN BY HIS METAL FILLINGS

HE HAS NO CHOICE

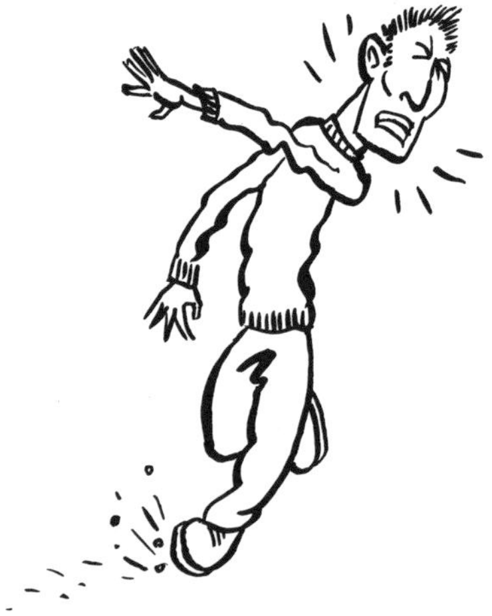

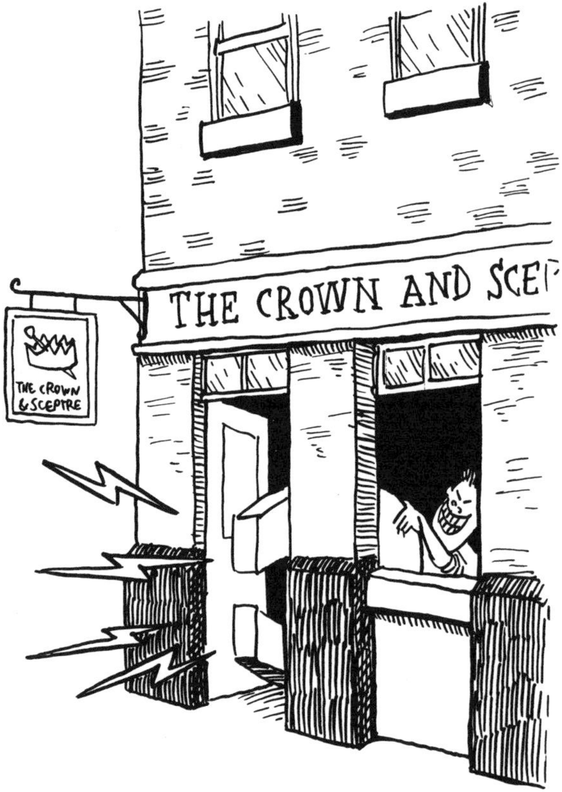
THE CROWN AND SCEP
THE CROWN & SCEPTRE

THERE USED TO BE A SHIP IN THAT BOTTLE

BUT IT SANK

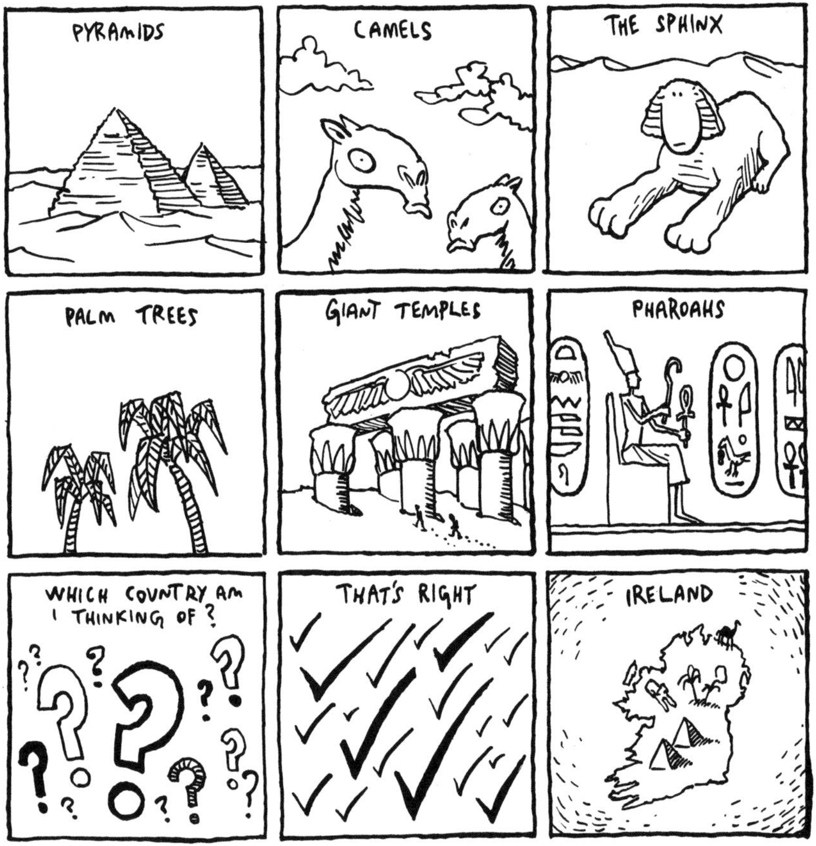
PYRAMIDS
CAMELS
THE SPHINX
PALM TREES
GIANT TEMPLES
PHAROAHS
WHICH COUNTRY AM I THINKING OF?
THAT'S RIGHT
IRELAND

YOUR DAD IS REALLY A YETI
HE SHAVES HIS ENTIRE BODY EVERY MORNING

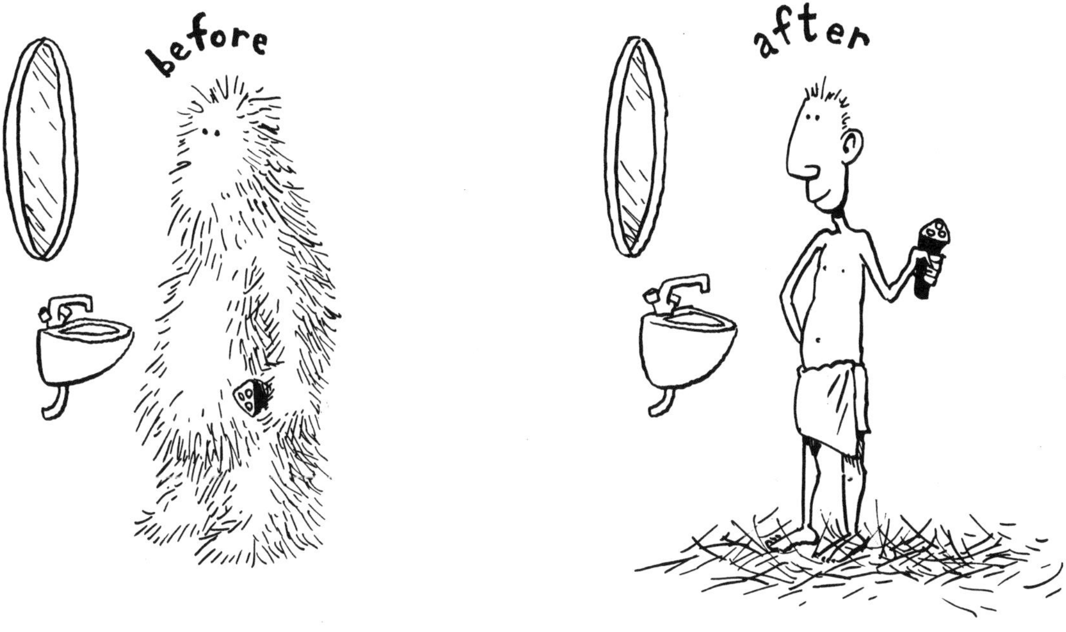
before
after

"JACK"

CAPTAIN JACK WENDOVER (1715 –1763) LOST MORE BODY PARTS THAN ANY OTHER PIRATE IN HISTORY

TWO IN EVERY FORTY THOUSAND
CARS LEAVE THE FACTORY
AS "SIAMESE CARS"

IF THEY SHARE AN AXLE
THEY CAN NEVER BE SEPARATED

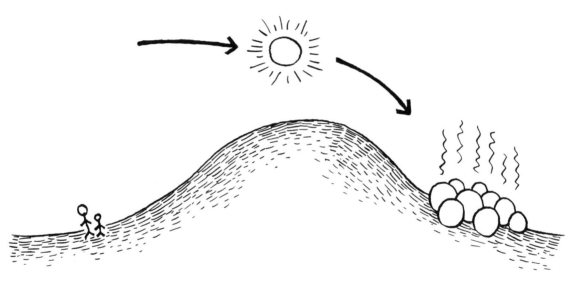

A NEW SUN GOES OVER EVERY DAY
THERE'S A BIG PILE OF THEM ON
THE OTHER SIDE OF THAT HILL

WHEN THEY COOL DOWN PEOPLE
CUT THEM INTO BLOCKS AND
THAT'S WHERE WE GET MARGARINE FROM

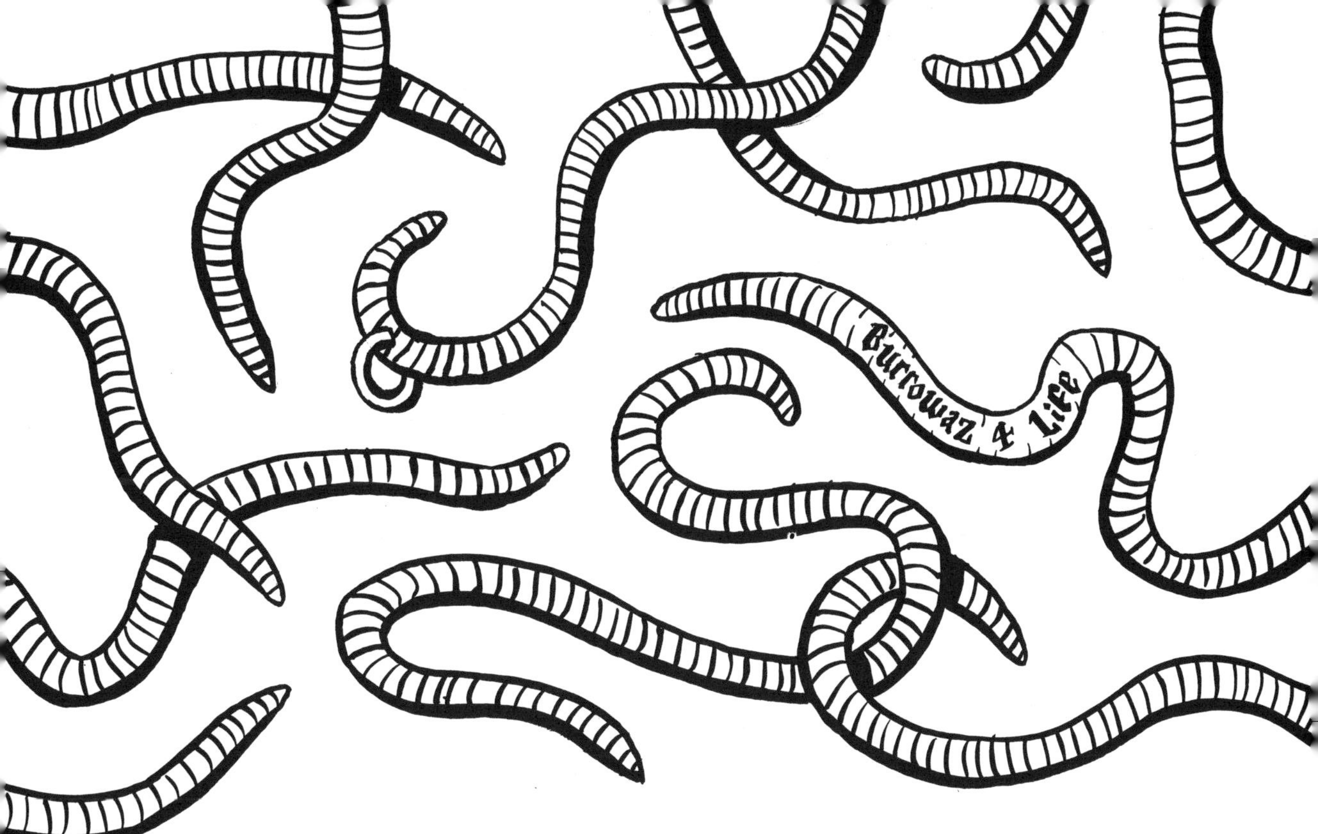
Burrowaz 4 Life

ONE IN EIGHT EARTHWORMS HAVE PIERCINGS
ONE IN TWENTY HAVE TATTOOS

MOST BIRDS WEAR PARACHUTES IN CASE THEY SUDDENLY FORGET HOW TO FLY

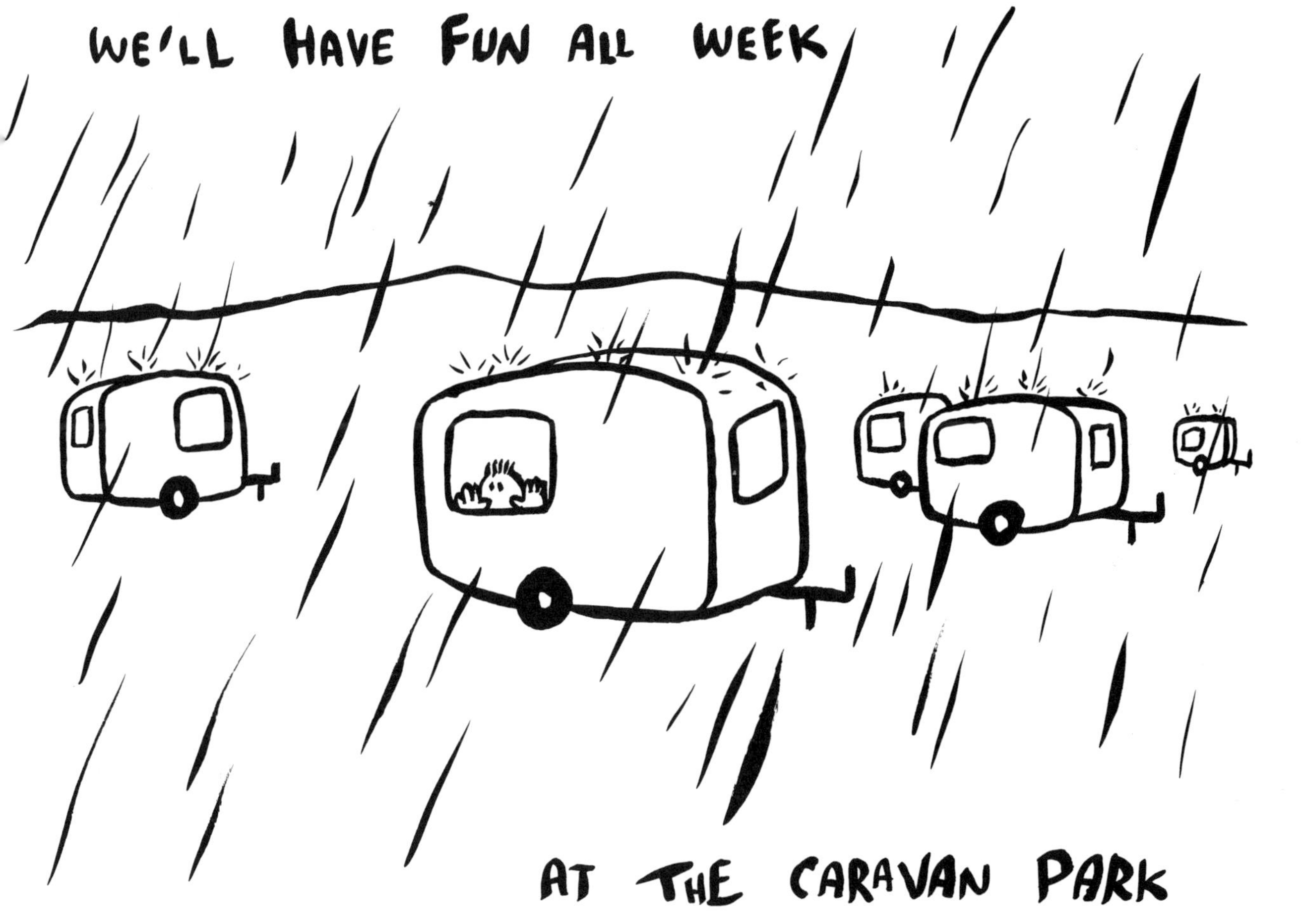
WE'LL HAVE FUN ALL WEEK
AT THE CARAVAN PARK

eggs talk to each other after you shut the fridge door

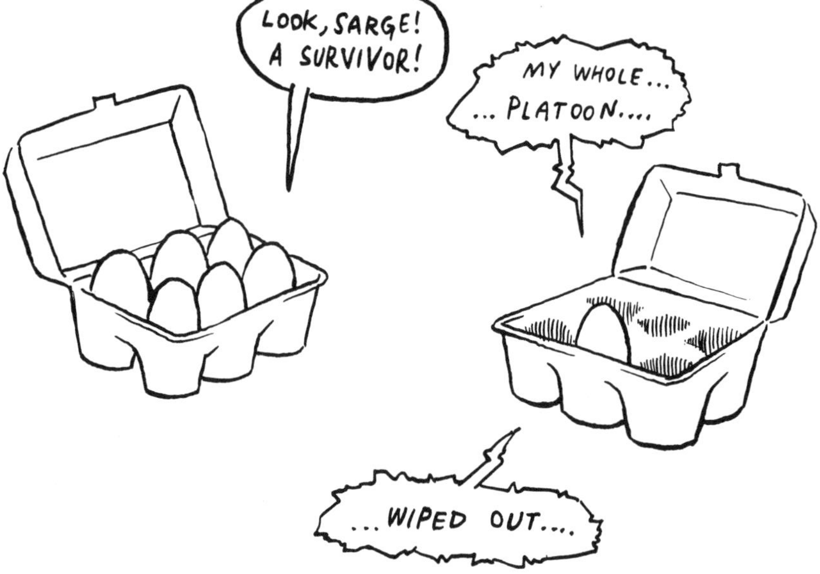
LOOK, SARGE! A SURVIVOR!
MY WHOLE... ...PLATOON....
...WIPED OUT....

THE WILD WEST WAS ONLY
TEN BY EIGHT FEET WIDE

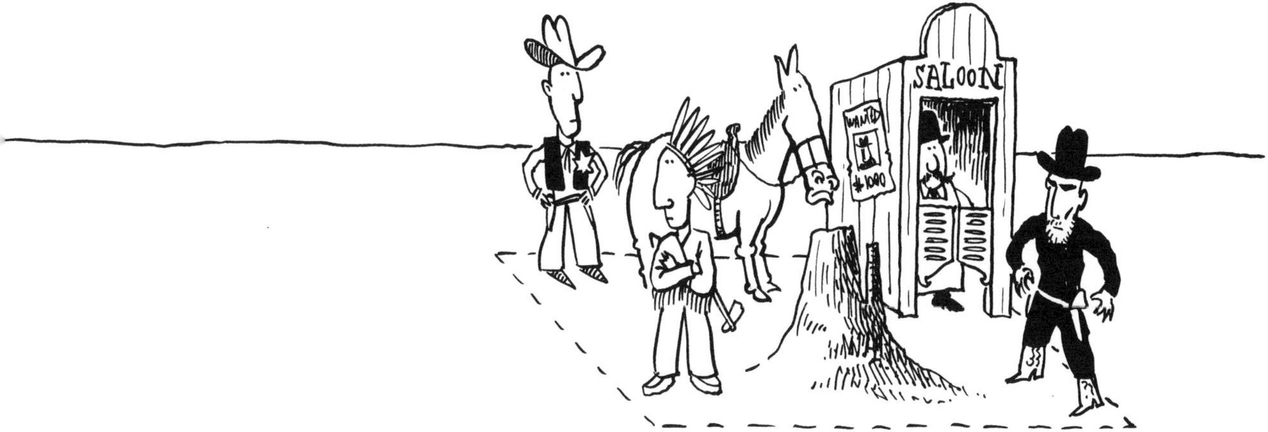
SALOON
WANTED
$1000

SLUGS
are just snails who've been mugged by other snails

If you ring the number of a house where you used to live you can talk to THE PAST VERSION OF YOURSELF

Never tell the THE PAST VERSION OF YOURSELF who is calling

NOTE: anyone who rings you and says 'sorry, wrong number' is almost certainly you from the future

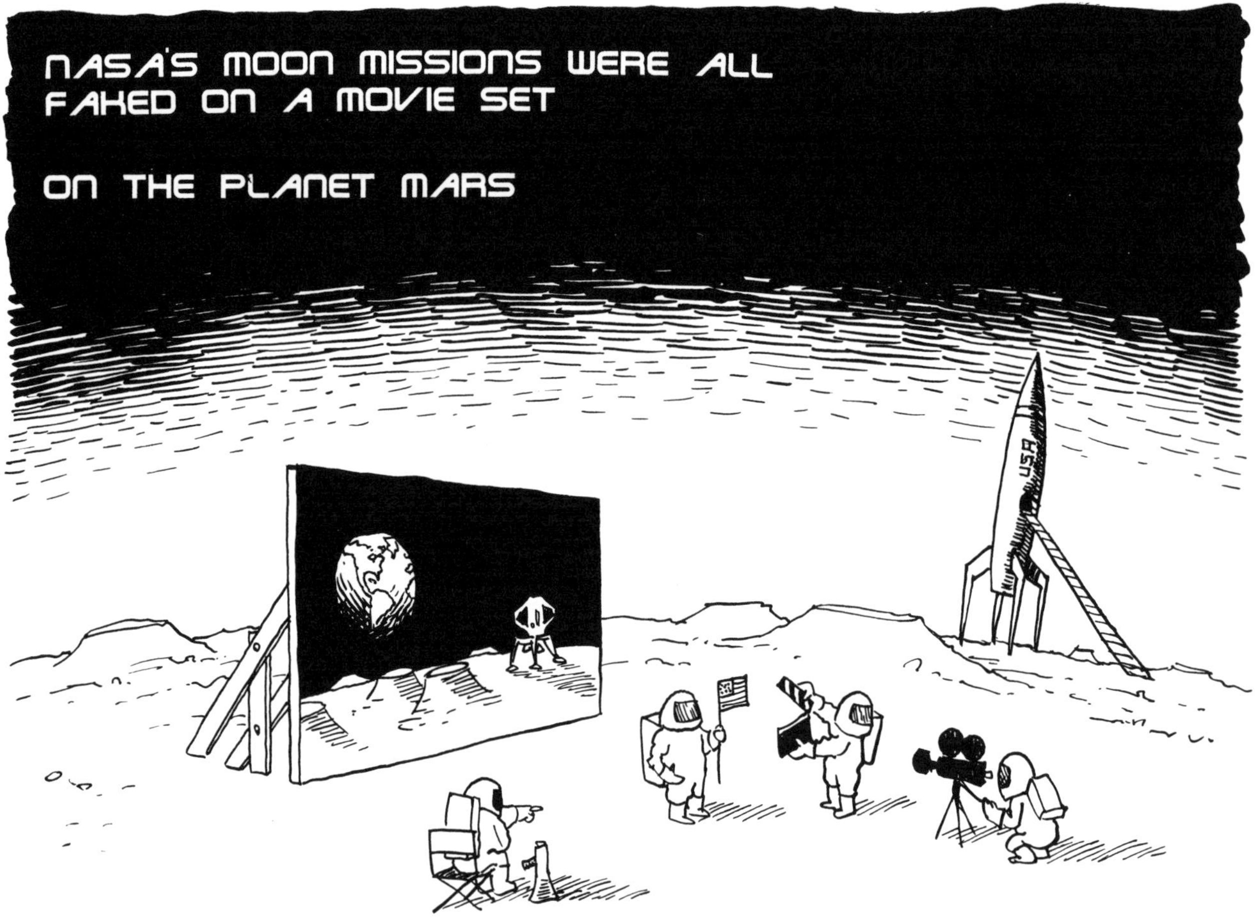
NASA'S MOON MISSIONS WERE ALL FAKED ON A MOVIE SET
ON THE PLANET MARS
USA

WE'LL GIVE YOU A PONY
IF YOU CLEAN
THE CAR

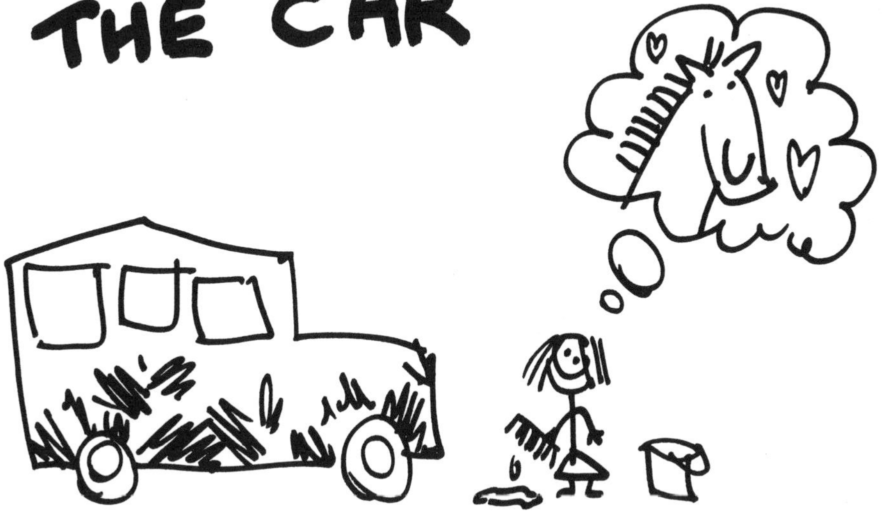

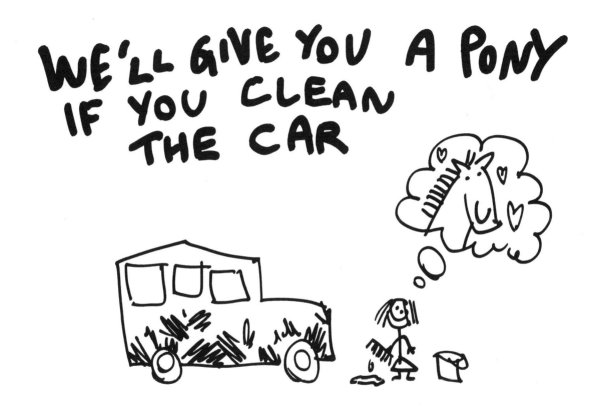

orange-hatted witches

always forget to
read road signs

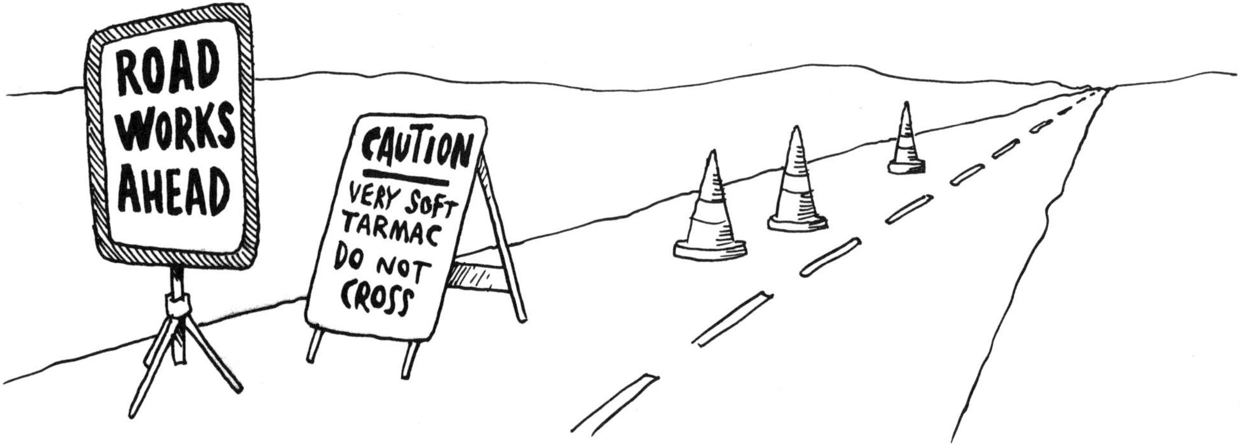
ROAD WORKS AHEAD
CAUTION
VERY SOFT TARMAC DO NOT CROSS

KEEP A CHICKEN NUGGET IN A SHOE BOX, LEAVE IT SOME
WATER AND CORN, AND SOON IT WILL GROW INTO A LIVE CHICKEN

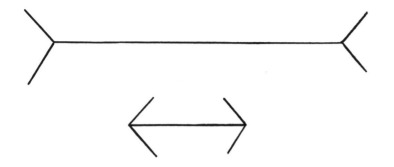

LOOK AT THE TWO HORIZONTAL LINES ON THIS PAGE. **WHICH ONE IS LONGER?**

THE CORRECT ANSWER IS **NEITHER.** IF YOU THINK THE TOP ONE IS LONGER THAT'S JUST AN OPTICAL ILLUSION.

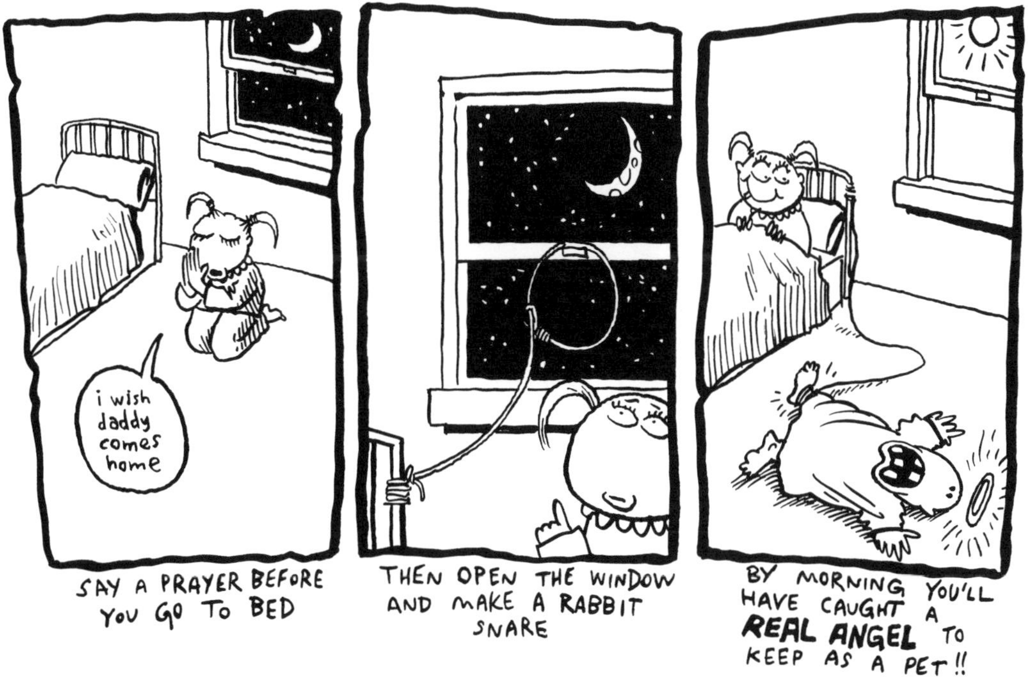
i wish daddy comes home
SAY A PRAYER BEFORE YOU GO TO BED
THEN OPEN THE WINDOW AND MAKE A RABBIT SNARE
BY MORNING YOU'LL HAVE CAUGHT A **REAL ANGEL** TO KEEP AS A PET!!

the statue of liberty switches hands when her torch arm gets tired
she only does it when no-one's looking

1951   1977   1998

the next time should be in about twelve years

WHEN YOU REACH
TWELVE OR SO, YOU WILL
GROW PUBIC HAIR AND
YOUR SKIN MAY GET SPOTTY

AND YOUR NOSE
WILL GROW TINY,
SHARP RETRACTABLE
TEETH CALLED
"DENTICLES"

YOUR DAD IS A SUPER-HERO

>He was bitten by a radioactive MAN, giving him all the powers of a MAN

>His super-hero name is 'MAN-MAN'

>His super-hero costume is jeans and a shirt from Gap

>His arch-nemesis is called 'All The Stuff That Needs Doing'

>Thrill to his exploits!

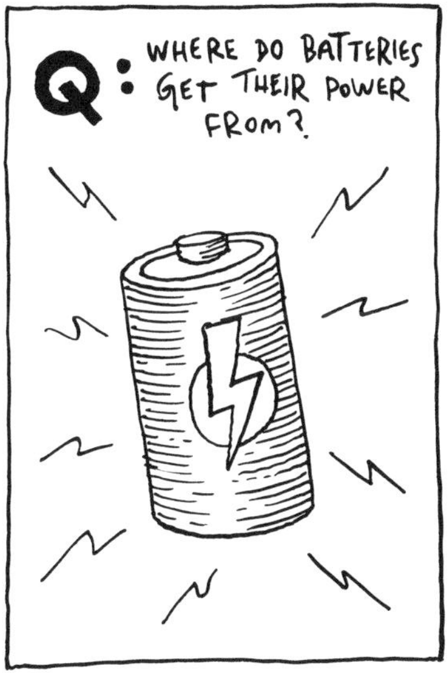
Q: WHERE DO BATTERIES GET THEIR POWER FROM?

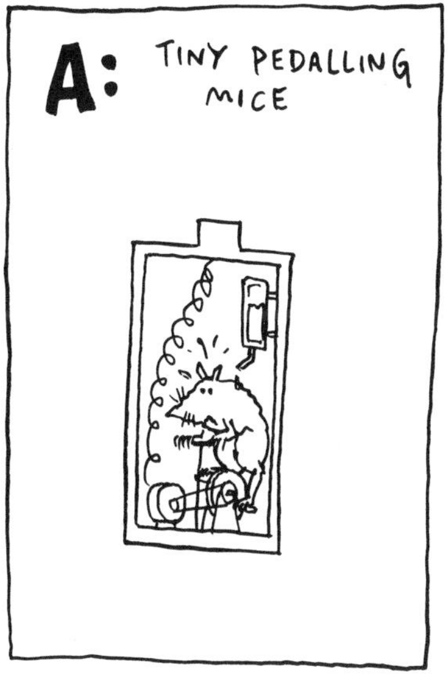
A: TINY PEDALLING MICE

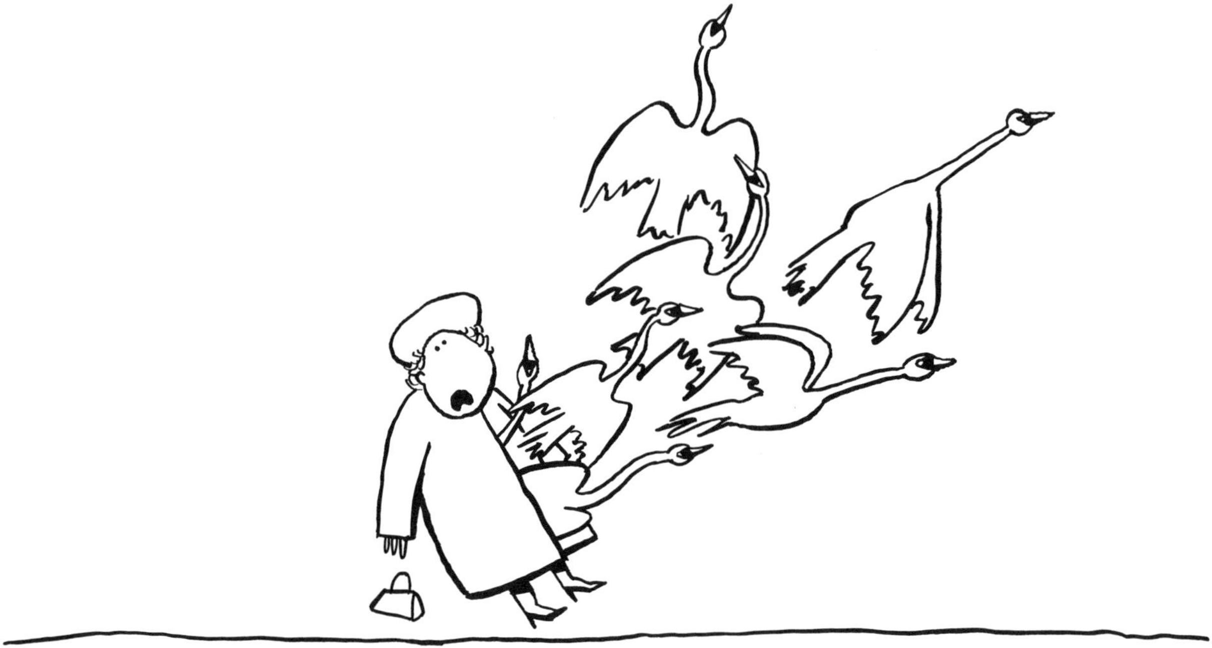

if you saw the queen split open
you'd see she's full of swans

IF YOU STICK YOUR HAND DOWN THE TOILET

IT COMES OUT OF A TOILET IN CHINA

TRY WAVING

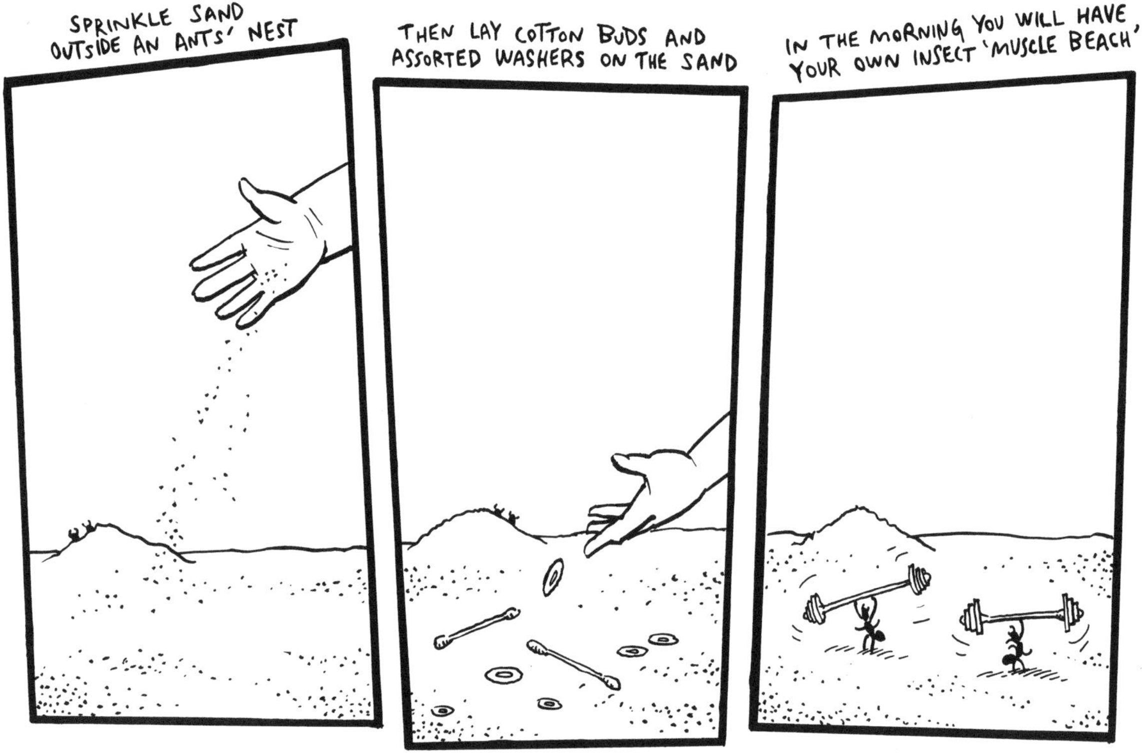
SPRINKLE SAND OUTSIDE AN ANTS' NEST
THEN LAY COTTON BUDS AND ASSORTED WASHERS ON THE SAND
IN THE MORNING YOU WILL HAVE YOUR OWN INSECT 'MUSCLE BEACH'

THAT ROAD SIGN MEANS
"BE VERY QUIET
IN THE CAR"

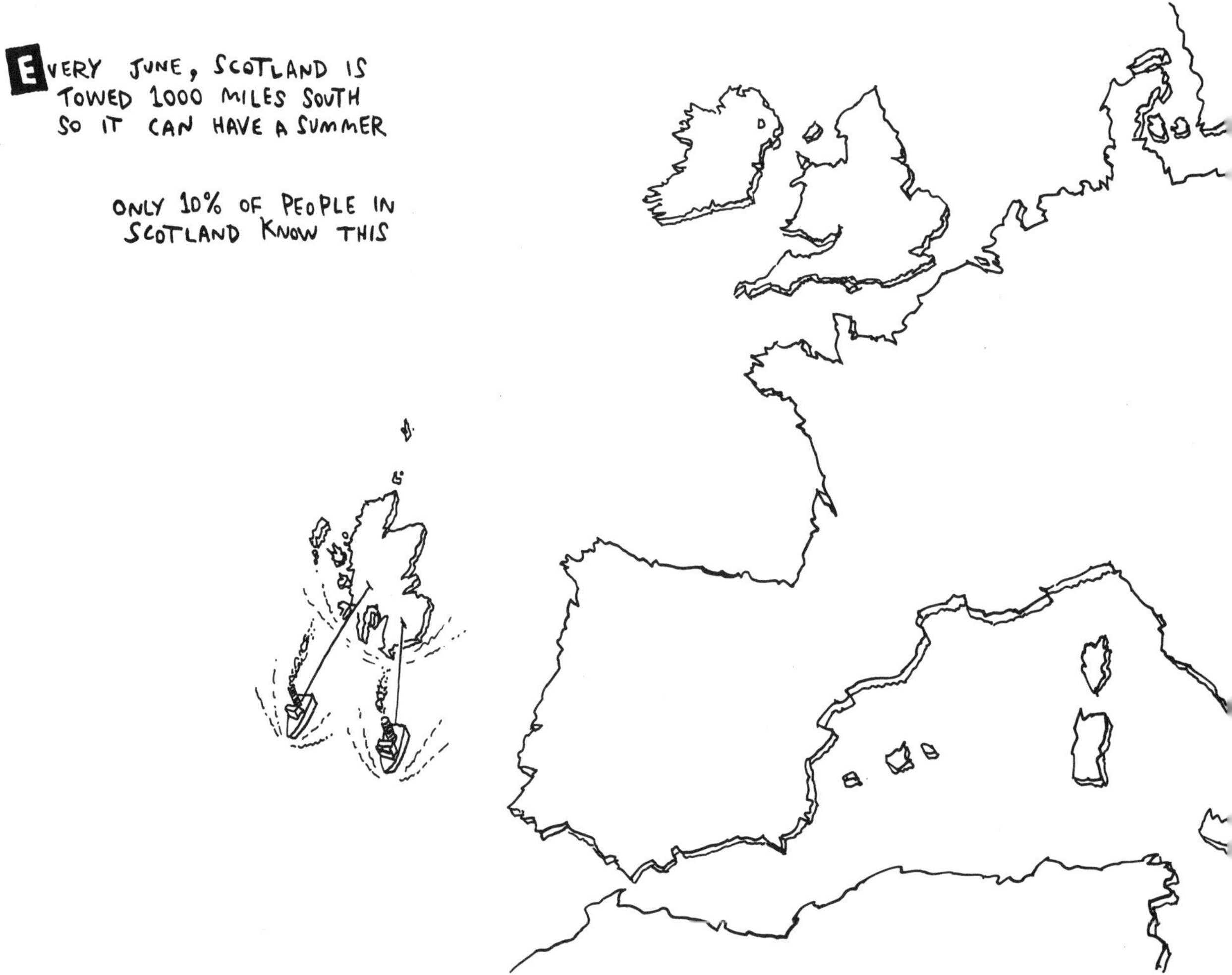
EVERY JUNE, SCOTLAND IS TOWED 1000 MILES SOUTH SO IT CAN HAVE A SUMMER
ONLY 10% OF PEOPLE IN SCOTLAND KNOW THIS

IF YOU UTTER THE TRIGGER WORD "BADMINTON"
TO YOUR GRANDMA

HER ORIGINAL PROGRAMMING WILL ACTIVATE
AND SHE WILL KILL ALL HUMANS

THE BEST COMPUTERS IN THE WORLD CAN BEAT ANYONE AT HUNGRY HUNGRY HIPPOS

EVEN RUSSIAN GRANDMASTERS

FATHER CHRISTMAS IS HIDING IN THE PAKISTAN/AFGHANISTAN BORDER REGION, NEVER SLEEPING IN THE SAME PLACE FOR TWO NIGHTS RUNNING

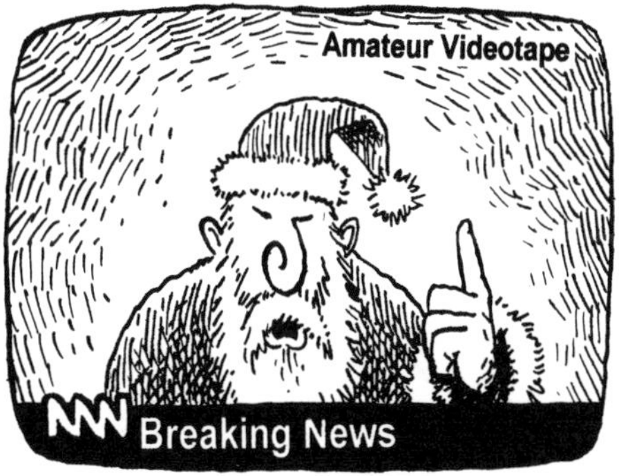
Amateur Videotape
Breaking News

HE'S ON THE CIA'S TEN MOST WANTED LIST

SOME PEOPLE SAY DELTA FORCE HAVE ALREADY KILLED HIM

THEY DIDN'T STOP DAD FROM DRIVING
HE'S JUST GIVING HIS ARMS A REST

FOR TWO YEARS

ALL THE OTHER SHEPHERDS IN THE NATIVITY PLAY ARE GETTING APPEARANCE MONEY

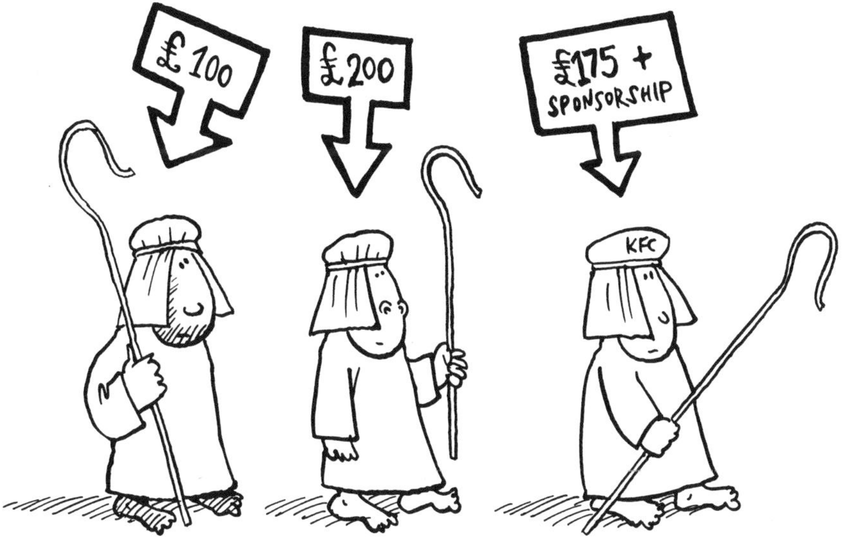
£100
£200
£175 +
SPONSORSHIP
KFC

JUMBO JETS RAISE THEIR YOUNG IN NESTS IN THE HIMALAYAS

THE PARENTS FLY UP TO 3000 MILES TO GATHER NOURISHMENT FOR THE FAST-GROWING "JUMBLETS"

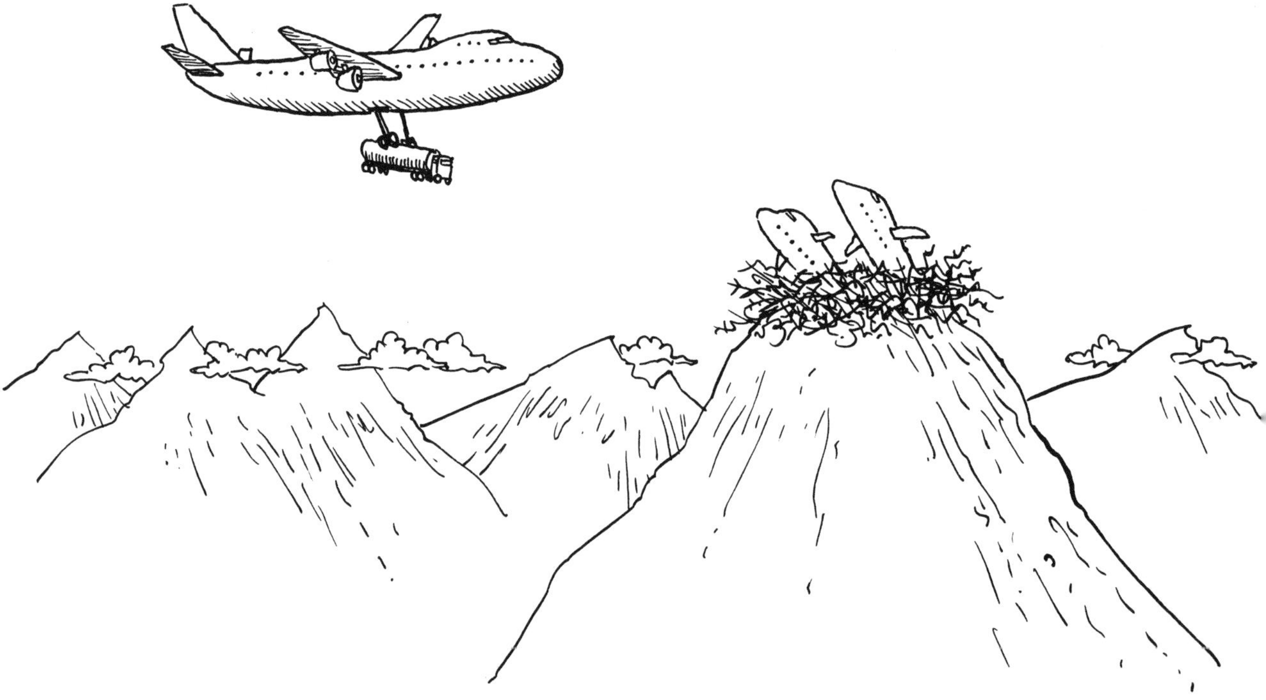

IT'S COMPLETELY IMPOSSIBLE TO TOUCH YOUR OWN NOSE SO DON'T EVEN TRY

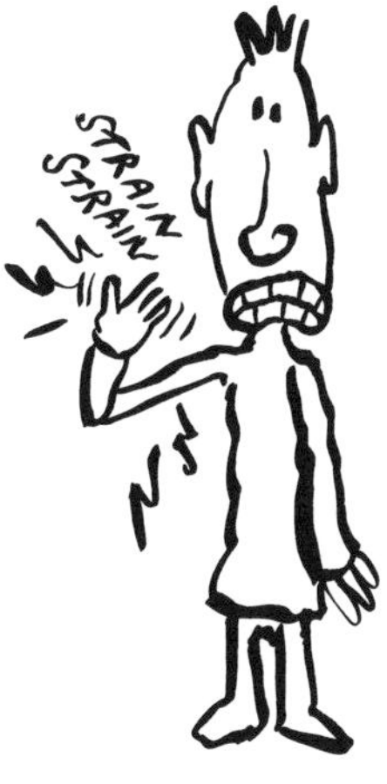
STRAIN
STRAIN

CLOWNS ARE MADE PURELY
FROM THE CHEMICAL ELEMENT
"CLOWN" (SYMBOL Cw,
ATOMIC WEIGHT 15)

THIS IS AN ATOM OF
CLOWN MAGNIFIED
3,000,000 TIMES

HAMBURGERS IN THE WILD LIVE IN DESERT COLONIES

THEY HIDE UNDER ROCKY OVERHANGS TO AVOID COOKING
THEMSELVES IN THE HEAT OF THE DAY

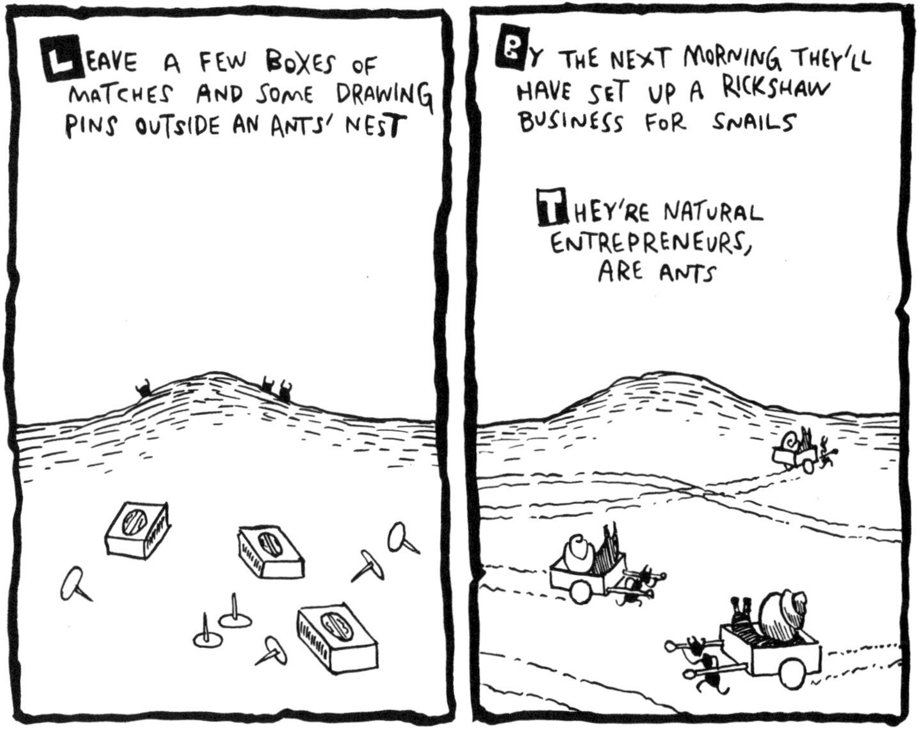
LEAVE A FEW BOXES OF MATCHES AND SOME DRAWING PINS OUTSIDE AN ANTS' NEST
BY THE NEXT MORNING THEY'LL HAVE SET UP A RICKSHAW BUSINESS FOR SNAILS
THEY'RE NATURAL ENTREPRENEURS, ARE ANTS

WHEN SOMEONE SHAVES OFF A BEARD
IT GOES TO BEARD HEAVEN

ALL BALLOONS HAVE A REFLECTION OF A WINDOW IN THEM *EVEN WHEN THERE IS NO WINDOW NEARBY*

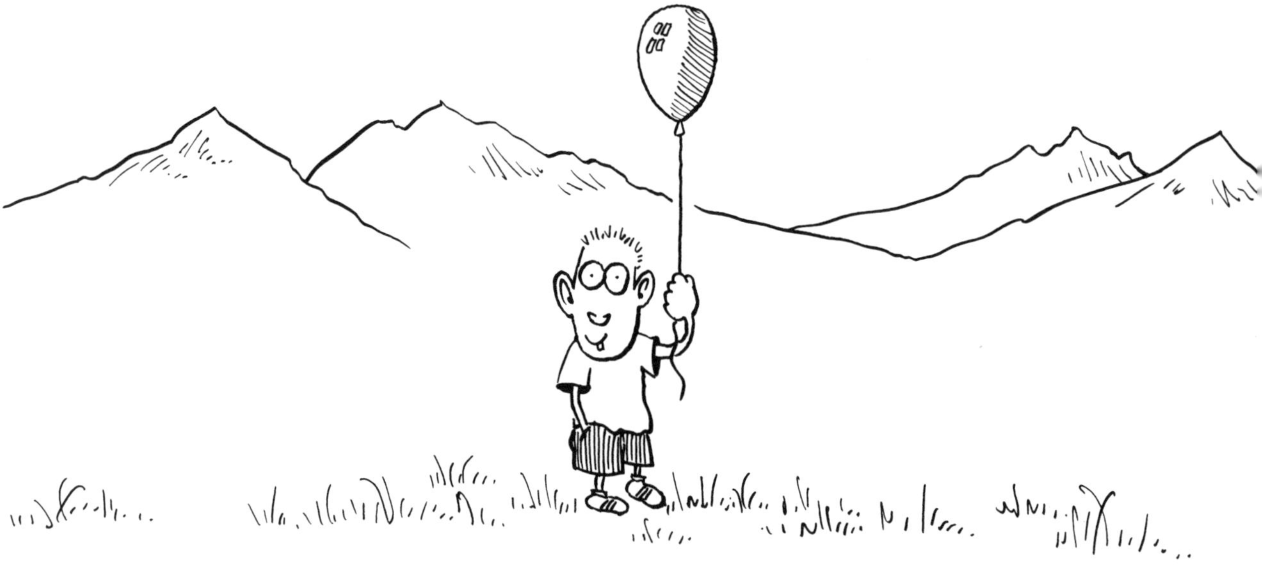

people who wear scarves

are just trying to hide the fact that they've got heads but no necks

THE FASTEST RECORDED 100 METRE
TIME IS 4.8 SECONDS BY MIGUEL
PIÑON IN THE 2000 OLYMPICS

HIS MEDAL WAS LATER CONFISCATED AFTER
A RANDOM TEST SHOWED UP AN ILLEGAL
NUMBER OF LEGS

> CAT POOs ARE WORTH £300 EACH
> COLLECT THEM WITH TONGS
> WHEN YOU'VE GOT FIFTY, TAKE THEM TO THE
   POST OFFICE AND CLAIM YOUR MONEY

YOU KNOW MY MUG IN THE KITCHEN? THE ONE THAT SAYS

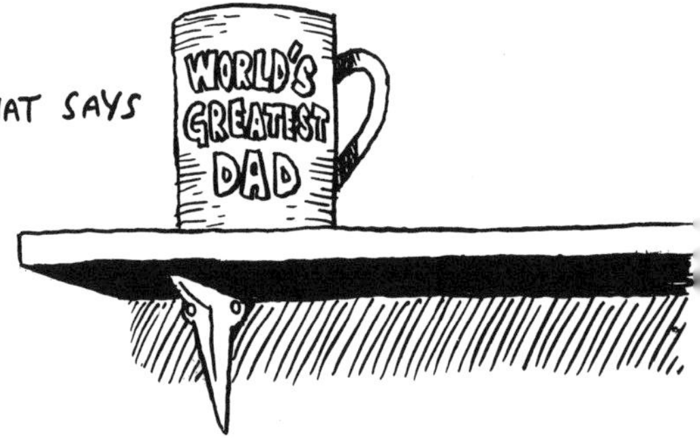
WORLD'S GREATEST DAD

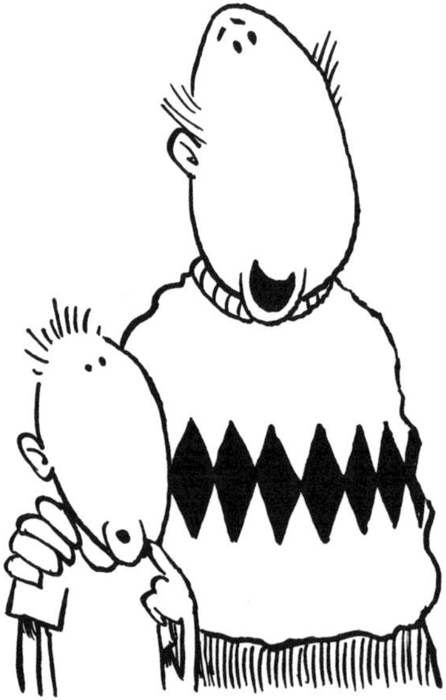

THERE ARE ONLY THREE IN EXISTENCE

THEY ARE AWARDED JUST ONCE EVERY 100 YEARS

I KNOW YOU DIDN'T SEE ANY GHOSTS WHEN WE VISITED THE CASTLE

T HAT'S BECAUSE THEY WERE ALL ON THEIR FAG BREAK

WE DIDN'T HAVE I-PODS WHEN I WAS YOUR AGE

SO WE ALL HAD 20 PIECE MARCHING BANDS
WITH 10,000 SONGS MEMORISED

if you spin round really fast and then stop your face will skid round to the back of your head

IF YOU BREAK THE LAW OF GRAVITY THE PENALTY IS HANGING

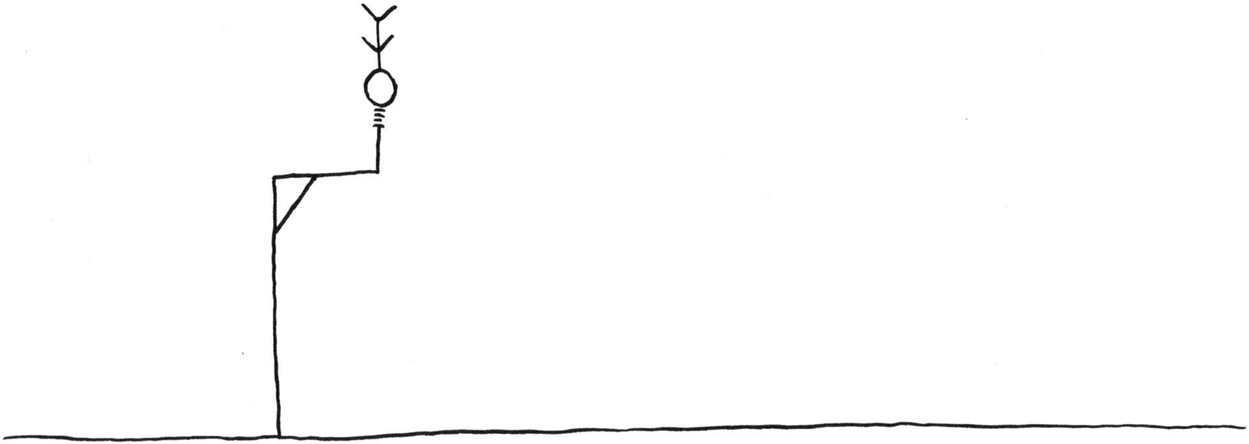

sometimes a daddy mole and a mummy giraffe have babies

though it's generally discouraged

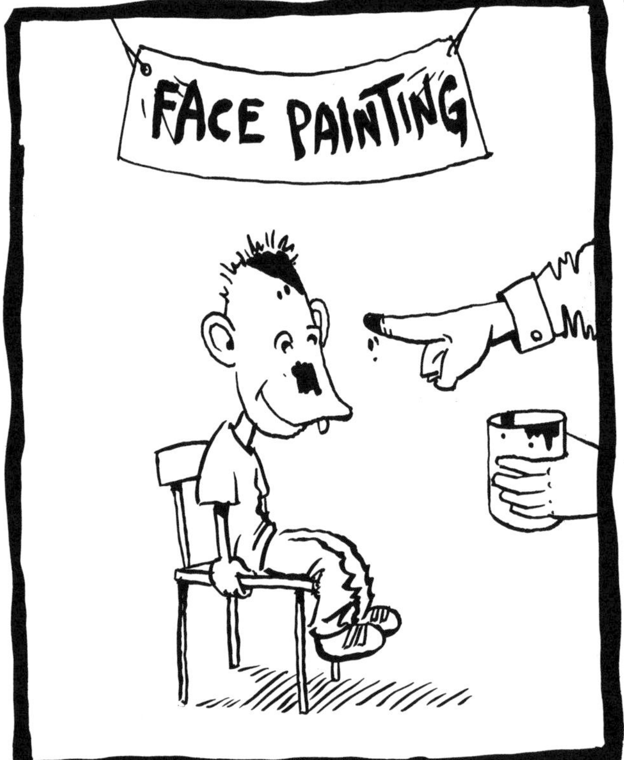
FACE PAINTING

THERE:

I'VE
DONE
YOU
AS
SPIDERMAN

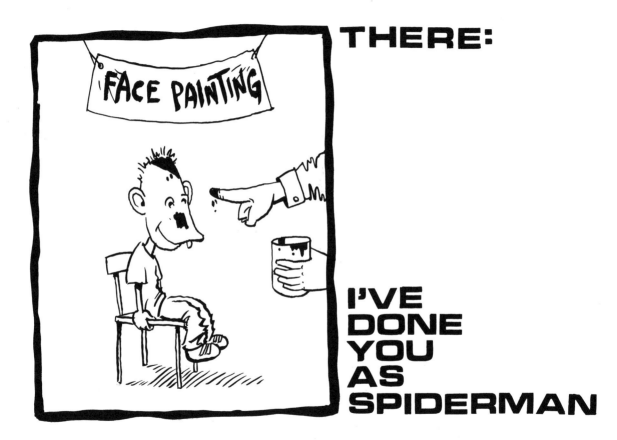

NOW GO AND PLAY NICELY
AND NEVER EVER TELL FIBS